DEESIDE AND THE MEARNS *and*

AN ILLUSTRATED ARCHITECTURAL GUIDE

Deeside and the Mearns must be one of the most diverse areas of the country, whether examined by its geology or its geography. From highland stream to mature river valley and rich farmland to rugged coast, it encompasses virtually every facet of rural life. The architecture and the area's social history is split – like the region itself – by the Highland Fault.

Steeped in history, the area has produced famous sons who have had an enduring effect on all our lives, whether in industry, culture or literature. Robert Thompson, inventor of the pneumatic tyre, Patrick Geddes founder of modern planning philosophy and Lewis Grassic Gibbon are all natives. However, our most famous resident, Queen Victoria, spawned an industry where the effects are still central to the area's economy. Balmoral is known the world over, but Deeside and the Mearns is also home to some of the more interesting fortalices of Scotland, whether garrison castles, pre-enlightenment chateaux or bonnet lairds' houses.

On arriving at Balmoral, Queen Victoria wrote: *All seemed to breathe freedom and peace, and to make one forget the world and its sad turmoils*. That sense of freedom is still evident today, and, unlike most areas of Scotland, Deeside and the Mearns is virtually devoid of urban architecture. It is more difficult – and consequently more rewarding – to seek out its fine architectural and historic specimens.

As a local to the area, I am sure this excellent guide can only enhance my forays into the heritage of Deeside and the Mearns, knowing that it will enrich many other visitors' knowledge as well.

John A Dickson
PRESIDENT, RIAS

D0097442

© Author: Jane Geddes
Series editor: Charles McKean
Series consultant: David Walker
Editorial consultant: Kate Blackadder
Index: Oula Jones
Cover design: The Almond Consultancy

Cover illustrations
Front *Crathes Castle and garden (reproduced by kind permission of the National Trust for Scotland).*
Back *Todhead Lighthouse (Geddes)*
    Inset *Tomnaverie recumbent stone circle (Jim Henderson)*

The Rutland Press
ISBN 1873190409
1st published 2001

Typesetting and picture scans by
The Almond Consultancy, Edinburgh
Printed by Pillans & Wilson Greenaway, Edinburgh

British Library Cataloguing in Publication Data.
A catalogue record for this book is available from the British Library.

Four sharply distinct districts – coastal, strath, lower Dee and upper Dee – make up the Mearns and Deeside. The sea coast, with its treacherous red cliffs colonised by fishing hamlets clinging to the edge of the abyss, is only breached by the gentle curves of Stonehaven and Bervie bays. Here the climate is notorious for its mean-spirited haar, the clammy summer sea-fog. Inland to the south lies Strathmore, the rich heart of the Mearns. This valley, sheltered from the sea by low hills, is dominated on its west side by the majestic outline of the Grampians whose colours change seasonally from blue to purple to orange and white. This is big sky country where magnificent cloudscapes, memorably painted by James Morrison (colour p.72), plume over the quiet fields. The River Dee forms two sections: lower region has poor soil, a broken profile with plenty of trees and few vistas; upper region begins at Banchory where the dank maritime climate gives way to bracing champagne mountain air. From here to Braemar the hills simply get higher and grander, mile by mile.

The four districts are shaped by their geology which has, until recently, dictated the local building materials. The hiatus of the Highland Fault runs westwards from Stonehaven: south of the Fault, amenable sandstone ranges in warm hues from sensuous raspberry red at Inglismaldie to sober milk chocolate in Stonehaven; north of the Fault and westwards up the Dee, rugged granite produces its own subtle palette of rose pinks from Cambus o' May to sparkling silver from Glen Gelder. In Glen Tanar a heady cocktail of quartz and many varieties of granite produce walls as bright as mosaics. With the two basic ingredients of sandstone and granite, masons clearly had different outlets for their talents. In the sandstone areas one naturally finds more intricate carving, fine details around doorpieces and even the occasional figurative corbel. In granite country,

Spital Bridge, Strachan.

Contrasting the Mearns and the Dee:
Chris liked the little place and the farms that lay about it, big and rich, with fine black loam for soil.
Lewis Grassic Gibbon, *Sunset Song*

*Land on Deeside needs a shoor o' rain during the day
And a shoor o' shite at necht.*
Local saying

Opposite *Fishermen in the Old Town, Stonehaven, c.1890, by Gordon Petrie (RCAHMS)*

Stonework detail, Ecclesgreig House.

3

Above *Roadside Cottage, Aboyne.*
Right *Quarryfield, St Cyrus.*

At first glance, the numerous crofts, single storey with a window on either side of the door, and perhaps dormers above may seem monotonous. One step up the scale, the two-storey house with three sash windows above a central door and windows on each side, presents an equally standard façade. However, as with most simple forms of construction, variations lie in the proportions. Minor features like the termination of a skewputt or the closure of a chimney (coved or flat) become significant. Equally, the details of coursing, dressing the stone and pointing vary according to the status of a structure. The ubiquitous dormer windows have a vocabulary of their own. The smartest have a carved stone pediment and may break the wallhead. Others may be canted, gable ended, pointed like a ship's prow, festooned with bargeboards or gracefully swept up the line of the roof: a particularly good selection can be spotted in Ballater and Braemar.

Clarack, Dinnet.

instead of carved door frames, there are timber porches made of knotty pine trunks.

In the rich sheltered ploughlands of the Mearns there are numerous old but modestly sized castellated houses from the 16th and 17th centuries, surrounded by large prosperous 19th-century arable farms with a couple of planned weavers' villages at Laurencekirk and Luthermuir. Along the inhospitable coast are the small fishing villages of Johnshaven, Gourdon, Catterline and Muchalls, with larger settlements developing at river estuaries such as Stonehaven and Inverbervie. Of these, only Stonehaven had a sufficiently sheltered harbour to develop into a town, the only real town in this book. Up the Dee, soil is generally rocky, thin and poor. Here the old houses are fewer but finer (Crathes, Drum) while the farms are mixed, with relatively small steadings for their livestock.

The progress of architecture has been seriously affected by the fortunes of the great families. Many have survived unscathed for centuries: the Arbuthnotts at Arbuthnott; the Irvines at Drum; the Irvine-Fortesques at Kingcausie; the Burnetts at Crathes and the Farquharsons at Invercauld. Others were rocked by the political rollercoasters of the Reformation, Civil War and Jacobite rebellions. While the Catholic Gordons at Aboyne survived frequent reversals of fortune, the Keiths' rise and fall was meteoric and disastrous. In the 16th century, they could ride from Caithness to Edinburgh on their own land, but by 1716 all their estates were forfeited and Dunnottar Castle was used as a quarry.

Poor communications held back development until the coming of the railways in the 1850s. Modern roads, generally following the rivers, totally distort the access provided by ancient pack-horse routes. Unnavigable and unpredictable, the Dee presented an obstacle to be crossed at perilous fords. The turnpike along

Geddes

Some historical imagination is often required in order to get the best out of the generally plain box churches. Most of the parish churches are dedicated to Celtic missionary saints, and are located on steep slope beside a beautiful stream, with perhaps a holy well or Class I Pictish stone nearby. All these are indications of a pre-Christian Pictish place of worship where water held a particular significance. One of the most attractive medieval churches in Scotland is at Arbuthnott, where the 15th-century aisle is like a jewel casket. Of the later churches, Maryculter preserves a fine set of 18th-century box pews while St James the Great, Stonehaven, and St Margaret, Braemar, have deeply satisfying revivalist interiors. A local characteristic is the fanciful bellcote of which a miniature tour-de-force is found at Tarland.

its north bank was only constructed after 1802: before then important communications ran north/south, crossing the high mountains of the Mounth (between Deeside and the Mearns) through several tortuous passes. Thus, places which appear remote today, like Loch Muick and Glen Tanar, were closely linked to the markets of Angus, over the drove roads.

Trains allowed new classes of people to invest in the countryside: rich entrepreneurs along the coast (Ecclesgreig, Brotherton/Lathallan) and sporting gentry up the Dee, from Queen Victoria at Balmoral to Cunliffe Brooks at Glen Tanar. Trains also extended the reach of the Aberdeen bourgeoisie to Stonehaven, Banchory, Aboyne and Ballater. Undoubtedly Queen Victoria's arrival at Balmoral in 1848 gave remote upper Deeside a new cachet and increased the demand for holiday accommodation there.

According to Fenton Wyness in *Royal Valley*, 1968, *Two tragic World Wars, the heavy burden of taxation and the appalling weight of death duties have all left their mark. Consequently the past fifty years have little or nothing to contribute to the story of Deeside's architecture.* A harsh indictment, but it is true that the capital mansions at Glen Tanar, Ballogie and Craigmyle have been replaced by modern alternatives. Other fine houses (Monboddo, Netherley) have suffered the indignity of 'enabling development', which has preserved the structure at the expense of the policies, and the possibly similar fate for Blairs is still undecided.

However, today, the situation is full of opportunities. Dedicated owners have rescued several notable houses: Lauriston, Tilquhillie, Fetteresso, Phesdo. Strict planning regulations have resulted in the successful conversion of many deserted steadings, mills and crofts. The dignity of the understated vernacular architecture deserves to be respected because of the visual harmony it creates with the landscape. So, forgive

Geddes

Geddes

Left *Parish Church, Fettercairn.* Top *Bellcote, Old Parish Church, Tarland.* Above *South Church Manse, Stonehaven.*

Manses are good and solid, frequently the most distinguished family house in the parish. Many were built in the fortunate period between 1820 and 1860 when the minister was clearly next to the laird in importance.

INTRODUCTION

The landscape, from the cliffs of Dunnottar to the peaks at Mar Lodge, provides an atmosphere of delight and wonder before a house is even visible.
The scenery's grand, the air, oh! it's charming,
Deeside being famed for excellent farming;
The mountains stupendous, and sweet heathery plains –
Travelling's pleasant, there's well arranged trains.
Advertisement 1866, S Martin, Aberdeen

an occasional swipe taken in this book at thoughtless and inappropriate intrusions, where modern buildings using imported materials and alien proportions clash unnecessarily with older neighbours. Equally, innovative and original modern contributions to the built environment are acknowledged. The challenge remains to develop eloquent and ecological new structures, which both respond to the scenery and respect the rugged existing stock.

ORGANISATION OF THIS GUIDE
The tour begins at Stonehaven, then through the adjacent parish of Fetteresso along the A92 from Newtonhill to St Cyrus. The second section, through the Mearns, meanders from Marykirk to Glenbervie, starting in the south and weaving to each side of the A90. The remainder of the book proceeds up the River Dee along the A93, from Banchory-Devenick to Lumphanan in lower Deeside, with a southern loop along the Dye and Feugh rivers. At Aboyne there are again two routes, the B976 along the South Deeside Road to Abergeldie; and along the north bank, via the Howe of Cromar, to Ballater and finally Braemar.

TEXT ARRANGEMENT
Entries give the name, address, date and architect (if known), with dates being those of the design of the building. Lesser buildings are contained within paragraphs. Appropriate demolished and unrealised buildings are included. Text in the small column illustrates the history and character of the district.

MAP REFERENCES
Maps are included for main towns and villages and are guideline only. Numbers do not refer to pages numbers but to those in the text itself. Where buildings are concentrated, space has allowed only a few numbers sufficient for visitors to take bearings.

Robert Barclay of Ury (d.1797), married to Sarah Ann Allardice, made his fortune in Jamaica in the 1740s and '50s. Returning to his family estate of Ury he began agricultural improvements, instructed by Turnip Townsend and Coke of Holkham. He removed 100,000 cartloads of stones, drained the soil and planted 1,500 acres of trees. He founded Stonehaven New Town in 1759, naming many of its spacious straight streets after his wife and children. His son 'Pedestrian' Captain Robert Barclay-Allardice (d.1847) who commissioned the Market Buildings, walked 1,000 miles in 1,000 consecutive hours for a bet at Newmarket in 1809.

ACCESS
Many of the buildings described in this guide are private and readers are requested to respect the occupiers' privacy. Several are open to the public or are visible from a public road or footpath.

SPONSORS
This volume has been produced with the generous financial assistance of Aberdeenshire Council, Grampian Enterprise Ltd and Kincardine and Deeside District Council.

Geddes

STONEHAVEN

Stonehaven enjoys a spectacular location; a crescent bay protected by the red cliffs of the Highland Boundary Fault to the south, and Garron Point to the north where the Grampians end. Settlement is defined by the rivers Carron and Cowie, entering the bay to the south and north. Its historic core nestles around the harbour which began as a small port for shipping wool and salmon, developing in the 18th century with grain, and enjoying the herring boom of the 1880s, with up to 80 vessels being registered there. The harbour grew after 1826 when Robert Stevenson, grandfather of Robert Louis Stevenson, blew up a huge rock at its mouth, and subsequently the double basins developed (colour p.65).

Stonehaven became the county town in 1600, replacing the less accessible Kincardine (see p.51). Early civic activity clustered in the narrow wynds by the tolbooth, close to the harbour. Its lack of Georgian grace was owing to the dead hand of the York Buildings Company which took over the estate of the attainted 10th Earl Marischal in 1716 and proceeded to strip its assets in Dunnottar and old Stonehaven until the end of the century. In 1759 Robert Barclay of Ury laid out the spacious new town around the Market Square, on the raised beach to the north of the old town. This allowed the architecture to develop during the 19th century from cramped tenements and fishing sheds to gracious bourgeois villas along wide airy streets. Lately, the Aberdeen oil boom has brought with it the familiar girdle of housing estates, which have sprung up during the 1980s and '90s.

Stonhaven harbour.

There is *a small harbour which they call Steenhive which serves only for pirates and picaroons, but it accommodates the Highlander for depredations. I take the liberty to call it stinking hive because it is so unsavoury.*
Captain Richard Franck, *Northern Memoirs*, 1658

Wood's Town Atlas, *1823.*

NLS / RCAHMS. C.McWilliam

7

The Old Town
Part of the harbour's charm lies in its varied texture, from the battered and worn sea walls and gnarled pink tolbooth, to the harled and gaily painted buildings along Shorehead.

1 **Tolbooth**, late 16th century
Built as a store for George, 5th Earl Marischal, it became the tolbooth in 1600. Crowstepped gables, external stone stairs, coved chimney and a wide loading door on the first floor (now a window). Now a museum downstairs and restaurant above, its worn sandstone is rugged but enduring. **Old Tolbooth sundial**, 1710.

Tolbooth and sundial.

James Graham, Marquis of Montrose, failed in 1645 to win over the Earl Marischal and his Covenanters at Dunnottar Castle to the Royalist cause. *Heichlie offendit, he wreaked his fury on Stonehaven. He fyris the tolbuith quhairin thair wes stoir of beir and cornis and the haill toun also, with the haill cornyairdis, houssis and biggings. He also burned all the vessels in the harbour. Outside the town Montrose uterlie spoilziet, plundent and undone the great houses of Durris, Ury, Glenbervie, Dunnottar and Fetteresso.* John Spalding, *Memorialls of the Trubles.*

Castle Street, 1965.

3 Old Pier, 18th century
Substantial three-bay, two-storey house with hipped roof, small windows and forestair to one side. Large sandstone blocks, evenly coursed, and chamfered corner to facilitate the turning of carts. Smart enough for a harbour master.

Marine Hotel, Shorehead, 1884
Victorian hostelry whose *c.*17th-century sculptured heads taken from Dunnottar Castle make you look twice at an otherwise bleak façade. The 19th-century **granary** has been converted into four storeys of apartments, harled on the front but with an attractive cliff-like rear wall with suitably small windows. The white painted façades of these two buildings give an epicene veneer to the old shorefront.

The essential 20th-century process of sanitising the Old Town has been at the cost of its former picturesque qualities. Much of the quaint patina in **Castle Street** and elsewhere has been sacrificed for practical harling, large-pane double glazing and excessive dormer windows. Only the derelict **5 Castle Street** is still single storey with its original pantile roof and shows the cramped living conditions in the original harbour dwellings. **Castle Square** flats, harled and with a lively roofline is a good attempt to retain the quirky angularity of the old town.

Albert Lane, 1950s, Stonehaven Town Council Stone-built council housing using vernacular features of crowstepped gables, dormers, sash windows and varied roofline. An outstanding development showing exceptional awareness of surrounding style, scale and materials.

Town House, High Street, 1790 Four-storey square tower with windows on each face, very conservative tolbooth-like form. Quoined ashlar, with timber balustrade surrounding timber belfry and leaded candle-snuffer spire. Pedimented clock 1896, barometer 1852. The townsfolk, requiring a dignified civic centre, paid a subscription *but it is to be regretted that this expenditure was made to effect nothing more than accommodation for the town clock.* Squeezed onto a corner, the tower lacks both the location and presence of a civic landmark. **Mercat Cross**, High Street, on older shaft, *c.*1645, head restored 1887 for Queen Victoria's Jubilee.

Top *Albert Lane.* Above *Town House.* Left *51 High Street.*

51 High Street, 17th century The earliest 'smart' house in town, for William Ogilvy of Lumgair. Three storeys, harled, tall and narrow, with bolection-moulded doorpiece with traces of interlace ornament and figure of man in frame. Corbelled stairturret now truncated at wallhead; 12-pane sash windows.

The ceremony of swinging fireballs along the High Street is carried out at Hogmanay. Although revived in the 19th century, the ritual probably has pagan origins. Similar to the Burning of the Clavie at Burghead.

Christian's House, 28-32 High Street, early 18th century
Three-storey-and-attic, five-window, ashlar-fronted house has pilastered doorpiece with 19th-century wrought-iron lamp holder on cast-iron standards.

Water Yett, 58 High Street, 17th century
Moulded archway leading to sea provided the historic access to the waterside, now regrettably walled up and harled over.

Former textile shed, Keith Place, 17th century
Three low storeys, an entire archaeology of openings, some bolection moulded; one end has crowstepped gable with grotesque skewputt. Cutaway corner on seaward side. Being converted to private residence. **Jubilee Court**, 18th-century warehouse for sails, converted to children's home, 1981. A sensitive restoration with swept dormers, pantiled roof and small-pane windows.

Top Christian's House. Above Former textile shed, Keith Place.

Church of the Immaculate Conception, Arbuthnott Place, 1877, J Russell Mackenzie
Satisfyingly complex and quirky in an otherwise plain location. The exterior pours extravagant details from Notre-Dame-le-Grand, Poitiers (blind arcade, western turrets and spirelet) and Chartres west rose window into a Scottish pint pot. Three-bay aisleless, buttressed nave, shallow projecting transepts, semicircular apse, in dark red sandstone. Fine entrance with wheel window, gabled doorway, tracery and arcades. Interior modernised and open plan.

J Russell Mackenzie, trained by Marshall Mackenzie and James Matthews, went to York for experience and returned to Aberdeen about 1859. He practised in Aberdeen with Duncan MacMillan from 1878–83 when he became bankrupt. He emigrated to South Africa and built the Goldfields Club in Johannesburg before his death in 1889. His finest work is around Queen's Cross, Aberdeen, where he designed the sandstone gothic Rubislaw Church, the Convent of the Sacred Heart school, Queen's Gardens Terrace, 1 Queen's Cross.

Church of the Immaculate Conception.

2 County Buildings, Dunotter Avenue, from
late 18th century
Terminating the view along Bridgefield, the most
serious classical building in town, altered, with
additions, 1822, John Smith; front 1863–5, J C
Walker. Its core at the back is a tall rough stone,
two-storey courtroom block with three arched
windows. It originally suffered from the *deformity
of a huge precipitous roof*, later remedied by the
present one with its cast-iron brattishing. Encased
across the front by a grave renaissance façade with
arched and channelled ground floor, an arched
porch with pink granite columns and balustrade
above. Architraves to the 11 square-headed
windows of the first floor. Stone balustraded
parapet. Modern east wing in matching sandstone.

3 Mill Inn, Dunotter Avenue, late 18th century
Seven-bay, red ashlar, *lately altered and improved*,
1842; plain parapet with raised panel in centre.
Snappy replacement six-columned portico adds
formality to a well-proportioned and
commodious building. Gutted and totally
restored as apartments, 1999, Gerry Robb.

St Bridget's Hall, Bridgefield, 1886, G P K Young
Visually complementing the effusive Catholic
church over the road, this hall displays a simple
gothic style with stepped buttresses supporting
roof topped by louvred spirelet. Timber cusped
three-light windows and jerkinhead dormers.

Arbuthnott Street
White Bridge, 1879, C S Hird and Blaikie Bros
Cast-iron footbridge with wrought-iron quatrefoil
parapet, a delicate contrast to the rest of the
street. Links St James' to the rest of the town. **No
1**, early 19th century, three bay, three storey, with
attractive wrought-iron balconies and moulded

County Buildings.

Mill Inn.

The Mill Inn was the old coaching inn
on the Edinburgh to Aberdeen route. In
1794 the 120 mile journey took 34 hours
but in 1830 Captain Robert Barclay-
Allardice organised the light-weight
coach *Defiance* to complete the journey
regularly in 12 hours.

No 1 Arbuthnott Street.

8 Arbuthnott Street.

St James the Great Episcopal Church.

doorpiece. Canted dormers with original glazing. **Nos 3-9**, late 18th/early 19th century, well-restored terrace of two-storey cottages with rubble walls and modern 12-pane sash windows retains a pleasing simple unity.

4 **St James the Great Episcopal Church**, 1875–7, Sir R Rowand Anderson
Magnificent red sandstone ark beached by the River Carron. Nave and lower aisles; semicircular apse at east end balanced by polygonal baptistery at west. The various heights and angles of the roof are effectively used to express the liturgical significance of the interior: the aisle roof is lower than the nave, transepts are expressed by the gable end elevations, the apse has a conical roof and the baptistery a prismatic roof. Outside, continuity is given to the elevation by a meandering stringcourse which links all the windows together – a purposeful feature repeated inside. Interior is robust Romanesque, round-topped aisle and clerestory windows, and round-arched, five-bay nave arcade with block capitals and wooden wagon roof. The huge west window floods the nave with light while the

slender five lancets in the apse provide a more ethereal atmosphere. The glass with images of saints in the baptistery is by Sir Ninian Comper, 1906. His father Revd John Comper was rector of the previous St James Chapel in Stonehaven (1857–61). Organ chamber and vestry, 1883–5, Anderson and Arthur Clyne; narthex and baptistery, 1906, and pulpit, 1886, by Arthur Clyne; reredos in Italian medieval style, 1884, Gambier Perry of London.

The New Town
Bridge of Stonehaven, Bridgefield
Originally built over the Carron in 1781 by Robert Barclay as the entrance to his New Town, widened 1885 and 1973. Below the **milestone** is a copy of the bridge keystone commemorating Theobald Barclay, the first of his family to come to the area, and the Mathers and Urie estates subsequently acquired by the Barclays.

5 **Carron Tea Rooms**, 20 Cameron Street, 1936, Colonel Tawse and Messrs Hall
Single-storey, brick and concrete Art Deco restaurant raised on terrace above period garden with original wrought-iron gate. Generous central bow with elaborate glazed windows overlooking balcony with wrought-iron railings, *the finest Art Deco patterned glazing surviving in Scotland* (C McKean) (colour p.67). Interior has decoratively panelled walls, Art Deco mirror, chrome, original light fittings and coloured tiles. Lovingly renovated in every detail, 1999–2000, by Hall and Tawse, the firm which developed out of the original construction team. Stylish exuberance matched by the open-air swimming pool, epitomising Stonehaven's image as a cheerful resort.

South Church, Cameron Street, 1868–9, James Souttar
Despite its bulk, this former Free Church fails to be assertive. Tall, gothic church with Greek-cross plan, large four-light traceried window facing street. **South Church Manse**, No 74, *c.*1844, James Henderson, two storey, canted dormers, rubble walls, ashlar quoins. Typical high-quality manse with fine pilastered doorpiece.

6 **30-32 Evan Street**, 1930s
Severe stripped Art Deco granite shopfront, backing on to Carron Tea Rooms at rear. Outstanding fenestration with bronze and brass glazing bars relieved by bright enamel plaques indicating butcher, baker and grocer.

St James Church represents the glorious triumph of the Episcopalian Church in Scotland after centuries of persecution. Because of their Jacobite taint after 1688, Episcopalian services were limited to five participants, and therefore usually took place in private houses, like Christian's House and the House of Ogilvy of Lumgair (see pp.9 & 10). 'Butcher' Cumberland *razed to the ground* local 'Pisci' chapels at Muchalls and Drumlithie in 1746, and in 1748–9 three local Episcopalian ministers were imprisoned in the Tolbooth for conducting services without acknowledging the king. Their devoted congregation flocked to the prison windows at night to attend services, and babies carried secretly in creels by their mothers along the tide line, were baptised through the window bars. Later, a small chapel in the High Street served until it became too small and the present St James was begun in 1875.

Below *Milestone, Bridgefield.* Middle *Carron Tea Rooms.* Bottom *30-32 Evan Street.*

Kinnear House, 33 Evan Street, 1854,
William Smith
Dignified and stylish former Town and County
Bank in confident renaissance: ashlar with
quoins, five window bays with moulded
architraves and balcony with stone balustrade
across three first-floor bays.

Clashfarquhar House, Ann Street/Robert Street,
1903, A Marshall Mackenzie
Five-storey, three-bay former Stonehaven Bay
Hotel under timber-fringed gables, dominant but
somewhat grim on the skyline, intended to
transform Stonehaven into a seaside resort.
Projecting bay windows on lower two floors.
A hotel until 1970, now a retirement home.

Clydesdale Bank (former North of Scotland
Bank), Ann Street, 1875, James Matthews
Imposing renaissance two-storey addition to
street. First-floor windows with consoled
cornices, bracketed cornice on roofline, with
panels in plain parapet. Roman Doric columned
porch faces Ann Street.

Market Square
7 **Market Buildings**, 1826–7, Alexander Fraser
Classical two-storey building forming east side of
square with projecting pediment in centre of east
façade, ground-floor arcaded ashlar piazza and
shops. Central tower has pilastered rotunda,
1827, octagonal clock stage, timber-columned top
stage and steeple, 1856, paid for by public
subscription. This dignified focal point of the
town (colour p.65) is disfigured by disastrous and
haphazard modern fenestration and signing.

Nos 12, 14 & 16, early 19th century
Three storeys, canted dormers with original
glazing, formerly Ramsay's millinery, outfitting,
costumes, silk mercer and draper. Blind Venetian
window in gable facing Evan Street. Lower two
floors fitted as a shop in 1930s. Doors have oval
glazed panels. Fascia with bold lettering and
volute at each corner, upper fascia embellished
with wreaths. Once more, a building in Market
Square with stunning potential is disfigured by
its modern windows on the first floor.

From top *Clashfarquhar House; Clydesdale
Bank; Market Buildings; 12, 14 & 16
Market Square.*

Robert Thomson, 1822–73, the inventor
of the pneumatic tyre in 1845, was born
on the site of **8 & 9 Market Square**.

Royal British Legion, Nos 26-27, 1862,
Peddie and Kinnear
Two-storey, symmetrical Italianate former Bank of
Scotland; outer windows bipartite with
colonnettes. Attractive creamy sandstone and

A Gibb

hipped roof sets it apart from the rest of the terrace, its clarity and strong horizontal lines producing a serene corner to the busy profile of the square.

Allardice Street
Opposite Edwardianised **Queen's Hotel**, early 19th century, is the former **Mowat's Tan Works**, employing over 100 people in 1888, once fine ashlar; converted to flats, 1974; painted, 1999, in cheeky postmodern primaries.

Geddes

Crown Hotel, c.1900
Jacobean curved-gable pediments on the dormers. North section remodelled from older building. A fussy façade made worse by the variety of windows and signs.

Geddes

Top *Market Square, west side, 1840 from Views in Stonehaven.* Middle *Royal British Legion.* Above *Crown Hotel and Town Hall.*

Town Hall, 1879, James Matthews and Laurie Renaissance, with pilastered doorpiece, segmental arches over ground-floor windows; first-floor windows round arched and keyblocked. Panelled parapet with urns. A dignified small building perhaps inspired by the parapets of County Buildings.

Carnegie Court and **McDonald Court**, 1980s
Cavernous rendered 'loggias' clamped behind bars create a sunless walkway in front of the entrances to these sheltered housing apartments. A grim antithesis to the joyful 1930s' Stonehaven style of the Carron Tea Rooms.

North end of street terminated by the hexagonal

Above *Belmont House*. Right *Invercowie House*.

Barely a trace remains of the Royal Burgh of Cowie founded by David I, 1124–53, on the east flank of Megray hill alongside the Causey Mounth road to Aberdeen. Footings of one wall of **Cowie Castle**, cling to the cliffs near Cowie Church. The burgh was razed to the ground during a raid by Montrose in 1645. The Barclay and Mather fairs were held up on the hillside in their traditional location until Captain Barclay-Allardice shifted them in the 1820s to his new town centre in Stonehaven.

Below *Cowie Mills*. Bottom *Wrought-iron gate, Stonehaven Open-Air Swimming Pool.*

tower of **Turners Court**, 1990s, and the discrete pantiled roof of **Somerfield Supermarket**, built in blending brownish brick.

8 **Invercowie House**, Barclay Street, before 1823
In the 1970s this was still the finest Georgian house in town but encroachment and asset-stripping have left it in reduced circumstances. Two storeys with basement and dormer windows, harled with granite margins. Two shallow bow bays with slender sash windows flank an arched doorway with sunburst fanlight. Generous staircase with iron banister sweeps over basement area to front door. Some panelling survives inside but many original features removed. The once remarkable terraced walled garden has been curtailed by modern housing at the north end of Barclay Street.

Belmont House, Belmont Brae, *c.*1820
Two-storey, three-window façade with central canted dormer and canopy over front door. Original railings frame terrace in front of house. Another fine Georgian house cluttered by recent solar panels, substantial conservatory, garage bunker and multicoloured artificial stone retaining wall in the front, contrasting with the old rubble and brick garden walls.

Cowie
Cowie Bridge, 1732, William Adam; replaced, 1827, probably John Smith
Three segmental arches with hoodmoulds and V-cutwaters, coursed rubble with droved dressings.

9 **Cowie Mills**, late 18th/early 19th century
Fine rubble buildings and three-storey pyramid-roofed kiln, clustered round courtyard.

16

Sympathetically converted to residential complex with new harled and quoined houses, 1990s.

Glenury Viaduct, 1885
On stone pylons, replacing the 1850s' wooden structure.

10 **Stonehaven Open-Air Swimming Pool**, 1934, Gregory and Gall
Cheerful Art Deco *station balnéaire* with colonnaded viewers' gallery and breezy wrought-iron south gate. Pool filled with bracing, heated sea water. A rare survivor from a glamorous era (colour p.68).

11 **Boatie Row**, Cowie, 19th century
This, and a small jetty, is all that survives of the traditional fishing community which grew up at the north end of the bay. The long, low terrace has completely lost its former character through the motley addition of new dormers and glazing, but the net-drying greens survive behind the houses.

Geddes

12 **Cowie Chapel of St Mary and St Nathalan**, dedicated 1296
St Mary of the Storms, with its rubble-built east gable wall and three Early English lancets is a rare medieval survivor. Lengthened in 15th century with rectangular window in west gable; late medieval priest's doorway in south wall. Church suppressed before 1567. Mort house at west end, *c.*1830. Notable collection of 18th-century gravestones depicting tools of the trade: blacksmiths, shoemakers, fishermen and masons.

Stonehaven Golf Club, opened 1897
Timbered balcony in spanking green and white paint has a nautical aspect suited to its location on the cliffs. Club House altered 1909, George Gregory Jr, architect; Robert Thomson and Sons, carpenters.

Geddes

13 **Cowie House**, from 18th century; mainly 1851–3, William Henderson
Characterful house set in windswept woodland, wings grouped round a court. North entrance front single storey and attic with gabled projecting porch and Georgian fanlight over front door. West wing has irregular fenestration on flanks and swept dormer facing court; south range, down the hill, has three storeys; sash windows. Walled garden links house to 18th-century stable court to north. Gatepiers, 18th century; south-east pavilion, 1930s. Alexander Innes of Cowie and Breda, 1728–88, and his descendants lived here until 1975.

Geddes

Dr William Kelly, 1861–1944, was a scholar-architect, a pupil and successor to William Smith. A great and observant traveller as his sketchbooks attest, Kelly made his Grand Tour in 1885 before entering partnership with Smith. His work for the Trustees of Aberdeen Savings Bank brought an early masterpiece, their Head Office at 19 Union Terrace, 1893–6. Equally characteristic, however, was his more self-effacing work: for Aberdeen Royal Infirmary from the 1880s until his retirement in 1928; as consultant to the Cowdrays at Dunecht; and specially his work in Old Aberdeen, repairs and restoration of such mastery and delicacy that they might go quite unnoticed. Yet Kelly never went unnoticed – a big man, he was such a stickler for good workmanship that apprentices and workmen went in fear and trembling.
Aberdeen: an Illustrated Architectural Guide

Right *Woodcote Hospital*. Below *Stonehaven Station*. Middle *Arduthie School*. Bottom *Mackie Academy*.

The Hinterland and up the Brae

14 **Woodcote Hospital**, Woodcote Brae, 1865–6, William Henderson
Built as the Kincardine Poorhouse, handsome classical, 17-window façade of coursed red rubble and grey dressings in lush riverside setting by the Carron. Tetrastyle frontispiece with pilasters and pediment.

Stonehaven Station, Station Road, c.1862
A Mediterranean entry to the seaside resort. Italianate, with two-light windows under arches and broad eaves; good cast-iron canopy and nicely cut sandstone. Thoroughly restored, 2000.

15 **Arduthie School** (former Mackie Academy), Arduthie Road, 1893
Three well-proportioned rectangular blocks in restrained classical style linked by spine wing at the back. Main entrances with pediments, triple windows on wings rounded with keystones. Prominent stringcourse links all façades with wings added in 1903; major rebuild after 1929 fire. Contrast this with the new **Mackie**
16 **Academy**, Slug Road, 1969–70, unadorned glass and rendered shoebox surrounded by windswept playing fields and approached by concrete slabbed path skirting the uncompromising bicycle shed. If buildings symbolise their function, this one suggests factory production rather than the seat of learning.

Heugh Hotel, Slug Road, 1898, James Souttar
This unusually proud mansion is a domestic version of Souttar's Salvation Army Citadel (see *Aberdeen* in this series). Asymmetrical baronial in shining silver Kemnay granite, brisk entrance façade with crowstepped gable and corbelled turret, main entrance tower expanding to crowstepped corbelled cap-house and V-plan

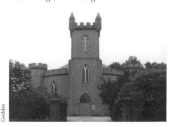

oriel; circular tall stairturret and right wing with pedimented dormerheads and circular corner turret.

17 **Fetteresso Parish Kirk**, Bath Street, 1810, John Paterson
Austere Gothick, harled D-plan with square central tower over entrance and octagonal turrets on each corner; crenellated parapet throughout and lancet windows with Y-tracery. Contains two important relics moved from Fetteresso Old Kirk: the ancient bowl font and one 17th-century carved panel from the old pulpit, now made into a chair.

Bath Street is a spacious leafy residential road with substantial individual mansions: **No 20**, *c*.1900, asymmetrical, dominated by Dutch gables and two-storey bays with ogee roofs. Arched front doorway with raised voussoirs. Mansard roof with red fretted tiles and round-headed dormers, an exotic addition to this stylish street.

Tudor Lodge, No 18, 1909, Dr William Kelly
Neo-Tudor, of fine coursed rubble with three half-timbered gables. Stonework, windows, moulded recessed porch and leaded lights show the academic attention to detail and craftsmanship characteristic of Kelly.

Bath Lodge, No 6, *c*.1800
Classic two-storey, three-window frontage, with canted dormers, in coursed rubble with raised margins. Large garden, partly walled.

The Hermitage, Baird Street, *c*.1903
Relaxed and informal, stepped plan, harled with ashlar dressings and half-timbered gables. Timber veranda with smartly turned balusters. Fine panelling and beamed ceilings inside.

Fetteresso parish forms an arc round the northern hinterland of Stonehaven traversed by the waters of Carron and Cowie and rolling through the barren bogs of glacial outwash between Netherley and Newtonhill.

Top *31 Skateraw.* Middle *Smokehouse.* Above *Elsick House.* Right *Berryhill House.*

NEWTONHILL

Once a picturesque fishing village, it has ballooned into a series of housing estates since the 1970s. The old rickle of fisher cottages has been mainly overdeveloped with unsightly large windows and excessive roof extensions. **31 Skateraw** retains its original proportions: a long narrow house with low pitched roof and a small window on each side of the central door, with tongue-and-groove panelling inside. Opposite, 18th-century **smokehouse**, a rubble shed distinguished by its kiln vent coming through the corrugated-iron roof.

18 Elsick House

Possible medieval origins with some very thick walls and low-ceilinged rooms; main structure, built after 1754 fire, two-storey, harl and slate, four-bay block with projecting gable-ended wings. Modern east wing, substantial refurbishment including porch, 1971. Home to the Duke of Fife whose family, through the Bannerman line, has held the land with only minor interruption since 1382.

Two good chapel conversions at **Cammachmore** (former Bourtreebush Free Kirk, 1843) and **Rickarton** where the original 19th-century box shape and generous window openings still dominate the design.

Berryhill House, early 19th century Standard two-storey, three-bay, with sash windows, ennobled by strong russet harl and two fine single-storey wings with embattled parapets. Walled garden at rear.

At **Aquhorthies** and **Old Bourtreebush** are two recumbent stone circles, *c.*2500–1500 BC.

Netherley House, late 18th century For Mr Silver, a successful colonist in the West

Geddes

Netherley House.

Alexander Ellis, d.1917, trained under William Smith (Aberdeen) and was in partnership with R G Wilson. He was responsible for St Mary's Cathedral, Huntly Street; St Mary's Episcopal Church, Carden Place; the west wing of Blairs College; and Corse House.

Indies; enlarged to the north west, probably by his son. *He built a genteel modern dwelling house and … made great improvements amid the gloomy waste which everywhere surrounds it.* U-plan, ashlar and some good cherrycocking. Projecting central bay with curvilinear gable, Doric portico and gablehead chimney is particularly crisp. Fine Adam-style plaster ceilings over the staircase and adjacent anteroom. West of the saloon is the formerly two-storey chapel with delicate lancet sash windows. Division into flats has wickedly cut the elegant stairwell in half, horizontally.

After the war, Netherley House was turned into a hotel with unsightly 1950s' extensions at the back. 'Enabling development' in the 1980s has converted the house into apartments and packed the landscape garden, originally laid out and planted with notable trees by Silver, with a motley collection of 'individual executive homes'.

Below *Cookney Church*. Middle *Cliffs, Muchalls*. Bottom *Woodburn*.

Cookney Church, 1885, J Russell Mackenzie and Duncan Macmillan
Built as chapel of ease for parishioners who could not reach Stonehaven, a lofty and cavernous landmark on its bare hilltop, with western transept and rose window.

Geddes

MUCHALLS
A few straight rows of fishermen's cottages parallel to the precipitous cliffs. While they remain single-storey houses with often excessive loft extensions, few original features survive on the street scene.

Muchalls Episcopal Church, 1831
Three east bays of nave; chancel, 1865, Alexander Ellis; porch, west gable, triple lancets and birdcage belfry, 1870. Elaborate corbel stops on chancel arch and good 17th-century carved chair.

Geddes

Woodburn, Bridge of Muchalls,
early 19th century
Former schoolhouse with gothic pointed door and windows with diamond panes, charmingly stylish for a diminutive cottage. Adjoining single-storey symmetrical master's house, with central chimney.

Geddes

Top *Muchalls from east by R W Billings, 1852.* Middle *Muchalls.* Above *Ceiling, Great Hall.*

A large house at Muchalls is shown on Timothy Pont's map of 1590, but gateway inscription states it was begun by Alexander Burnett of Leys, owner of Crathes Castle, in 1619, and completed by his son Thomas in 1627. The same team of presumably English plasterers worked at Craigievar and Glamis in the 1620s. *It is surrounded by its rook-tenanted ancestral trees. The surrounding bleakness gives this small patch a solitude like that of an island upon the ocean.*
R W Billings, 1852

19 **Muchalls**, 1619–27
On a breezy hilltop facing the sea, three storey, L-plan on older basement vaulting. A rare example of an original barmkin whose decorative bartizans, monumental inscription and gunloops complete a charming courtyard formed by the wings of the house. Stairtower in the re-entrant and turrets on most of the gables. Roofline punctured by massive chimneystacks. Great hall on the first floor of the main block has plaster ceiling with heraldic designs (fully tinctured) of the Burnett and other families, and heads of The Heroes in roundels. Coloured overmantle to fireplace decorated with the royal arms of Scotland and dated 1624. Fine ceilings also in the withdrawing room and laird's study. Perched on the edge of the terrace, rare 17th-century, two-storey 'banqueting house'. Repaired 1890, A Marshall Mackenzie. Muchalls bristles with stunning details applied on a relatively modest scale.

20 **Ury House**, 1855, John Baird
Roofless and abandoned after 1945, grotesquely affluent Tudor mansion in fine sandstone ashlar with sculptured details. Typical of Baird's overscaled work (see *The Monklands* in this series). Three storeys, gable pediments on dormers; massive mullion window beside the tower illuminated the hall. North front has *porte-cochère* and projecting tower with oriel.

Penelope Gregory

Old Ury House.

Previously the site of a late 17th-century house, L-plan, three-storey with circular towers (lower than the main roof) attached to each gable end, *an old castle built house having very thick strong walls*. In 1789, James Playfair produced unexecuted designs to remodel the house. The Ury estate, once belonging to the Barclay family who developed the New Town of Stonehaven in 1759, was redesigned for its new owner Alexander Baird, Lord Lieutenant, in 1855. The estate and most of its ancillary buildings, abandoned after the Second World War, are in a state of decay. The extensive park wall was built before 1845.

Wing with crowstepped gables added to east end, 1884, Alexander Ross. Garden terrace has channelled and buttressed walls.

21 **Rickarton House**
Friendly classical villa façade by John Smith with low-pitched roof added *c.*1830 to east side of older double pile house, set in deep mature woodland. **Rickarton Gardener's Cottage**, *c.*1840, harled and slated, with two gothic windows and picturesque porch. **Cheyne Farmhouse**, early 19th century, harled with ashlar margins, three-part windows and circular turreted central bay.

Aberdeen University Library

Auquhollie stone, 6th–7th century
Impressive Pictish monolith inscribed with ogham lettering. On a prominent hilltop above, **Raedykes Roman Camp**, *c.*83 AD, built as a marching camp on Agricola's campaign. Covering almost 100 acres, its north corner is most clearly defined, with deep ditch and embankment.

Geddes

22 **Mergie**, 17th century
Hidden in the braes near Slug Road, *It would make a cheerful summer residence for valetudinary people or fine shooting quarters for gentlemen of the chace* (sic) (G Robertson). Rectangular plan, with projecting entrance wing and stair added in 19th century, pink-harled and slated with ashlar dressings. Corbelled stairturrets on west façade and at the re-entrant angle. Original panelling with bolection mouldings survives inside. The bonnet laird's house, an unusual style, miniature in scale but high in presumption. Surviving 18th-century *plaisance* or garden, terraced with ruined pavilions.

Geddes

Fetteresso Old Parish Kirk, dedicated 1246
Rectangular box with gothic north-west doorway, rebuilt mid-17th century; north aisle 1720; birdcage bellcote with triangular pediments, 1737. The dedication of the church to St Kieran, its

Geddes

From top *Ury House, c.1900, photographed by George Washington Wilson; Rickarton House; Rickarton Gardener's Cottage; Mergie.*

On country churches generally, but especially Fetteresso, *c.*1800: *Nothing could be more mean in outward appearance nor less elegant in the internal arrangement, than the general run of country kirks. They were dismally ill lighted, and seldom being lathed and plaistered, and often without any flooring or pavement, they were commonly very damp and full of noxious vapour.* G Robertson

location on a steep hillside above the Carron Water and at the southern extremity of the parish suggests this was an early cult site. Good lettering on many 18th- and 19th-century gravestones.

The kirkton is a picturesque 18th-century grouping, **Old Inn** and **Old School** beside the churchyard walls, stream and bridge.

23 **Fetteresso Castle**, from early 16th century
A castle was recorded here in 1587, becoming the residence of the Earl Marischal in the early 17th century when the Countess, upset by the noise of seals, wished to leave Dunnottar. John Paterson converted the L-plan manor into a Gothick mansion, 1808, towering on a steep hillside overlooking the 16th-century beehive **doocot**, terraced gardens and orchards, *very fine and large inclosures with abundance of planting* (1722). The grand octagonal entrance tower acts as the hub from which extend at right angles two three-storey wings, capped by parapets and punctuated by lesser turrets. A service court and coach house completes the courtyard formed by the wings. Windows are pointed or rectangular with hoodmoulds. Gutted and roofless 1954; rescued and converted into apartments, 1992, by Bob Fitzgerald, dividing the building vertically; interiors entirely modern.

The 1587 castle was destroyed by the Marquis of Montrose in 1645, on his campaign against the Covenanters. A date panel of 1671 marks the rebuilding. In 1715, James Stuart 'The Old Pretender', under the protection of George Keith, 10th Earl Marischal, was proclaimed King James VIII in Fetteresso Castle. The property was forfeited after the rising failed and Colonel Robert William Duff extended the old L-plan house with its longer wings and Gothick façades in 1808.

Dunnottar Parish Church, from 1394
Begun by Sir William de Keith after being
excommunicated by the pope for impeding
access to the old parish church within his castle.
Present oblong building 1782, extended 1862,
remodelled, 1903, by G P K Young, turning the
old nave into transepts. Fine wooden trussed
roof, 1906. Small, gothic **Marischal Aisle** built by
George Keith, 5th Earl Marischal, 1582, heavily
rebuilt, 1913, by Marischal College, Aberdeen
University, in memory of its founder.

Dunnottar Old Manse, 1786
Two storey and attic, ashlar and slate, with
central gable, late 19th-century extensions.

Dunnottar House, *c.*1800 (demolished 1957)
Bald-looking two-storey classical, with Venetian
windows on either side of a semicircular portico
with Corinthian columns, for Alexander
Allardyce who made his fortune in Jamaica. A
sugar-fuelled extravaganza is revealed in the
delights of the Gothick landscape. Garden walls of
mellow local brick are mighty enough to encircle a
city. Diminutive **Shell House**, originally faced
with sea-cliff conglomerate, restored, 2000, by
local trust and shell artist Diana Reynell. The
interior was barnacled with rib vaults of sea
urchins and heraldic panels of scallops, conches,
and had a water feature lined with blue john.

Invercarron Tollhouse, early 19th century
Harl and slate, with semi-octagonal bay front,
strategically guarding both A92 and A94.

Black Hill War Memorial, 1923, John Ellis
Greek temple ruin of Doric columns supporting
entablature. Stark against the horizon, this
memorial links the sky, cliffs and sea, like the
Temple of Poseidon at Sounion, Greece.

Bricklaywaird Farmhouse, early 19th century
Two-storey, rubble and slate, on splendid abrupt
natural terrace.

24 **Dunnottar Castle**, from 13th century
Approached by a precipitous clifftop path,
buildings for an entire community are spread
organically around the site, clinging to the
periphery of the rock leaving a wide central space,
more like a village green than a castle courtyard
(colour p.66).
   Chapel (1), whose dedication to St Ninian
perhaps implies an early Celtic foundation, was

Sir Walter Scott, staying at Dunnottar
Manse in 1788, watched an old man
loyally cleaning the gravestone which
listed all those Covenanters who had
died in the Whigs' Vault in Dunnottar
Castle in 1685. This character, Robert
Patterson, became the hero in Scott's
Old Mortality.

From top *Dunnottar Parish Church;
Dunnottar Old Manse; Dunnottar House;
Invercarron Tollhouse; Black Hill War
Memorial.*

Opposite from top *Old Parish Kirk; Old
Inn; Old School; Doocot, Fetteresso Castle.*
Right *Fetteresso Castle.*

RCAHMS

Dunnottar Castle: above *aerial view*;
right *based on Slezer's* Theatrum Scotiae
1693 by an unknown artist.

Dunnottar is the most significant
monument in this volume and also one
of the most memorable in Scotland. Its
significance lies beyond the unbeatable
location on its precarious promontory,
relating also to its centuries of
occupation, variety of building styles
and teeming history. The comfortable
domestic buildings around relaxed and
spacious courtyards are an unexpected
contrast to the ferocious exterior and
entrance. The design of a long low
quadrangle formed by a row of lodgings,
hall and bakehouse range is unusual in
Scotland, more compact examples being
found at Tolquhoun and Boyne (see
Gordon and *Banff & Buchan* in this series).
*It is rather a village of dwellings than one
dwelling, it is a Palace and a Fort.*

A fortified site at 'Duin Foither' is
mentioned in the *Annals of Ulster* as early
as 681. However, the earliest evidence of
settlement is just to the north, where
Pictish stones were found on the stack of
Dunnicaer (see Beannacher p.76) and
where an undated bank encloses the
Bowduns promontory. In the 12th
century, William the Lion used
Dunnottar as an administrative base and
Edward I's garrison there was wiped out
by William Wallace in 1297. Rebelling
against Charles II's promotion of
Episcopacy, 167 Covenanters were
crammed into the Whigs' Vault with no
food or sanitation for six weeks in 1685.
Seven died in prison and two fell to their
death trying to escape down the cliff.
They are buried in Dunnottar kirkyard.

RCAHMS

consecrated in 1276. Probably lower parts of the
south wall and two small windows date from this
period, the rest rebuilt 16th century. At west end,
simple pointed doorway and large window above,
fireplace at east end. Licence to build the **tower
house** (2) was granted in 1346 but the L-shaped
block may not have been begun for 50 years. Store
in vaulted basement later converted to kitchen,
replacing a smaller one on first floor, adjacent to
great hall. Private hall on next floor, top storey for
sleeping. Window embrasures are frequently
provided with stone seats. Exterior decorated by
very simple corbel table and cap-house.

Miniature laird's house, **Waterton's Lodging**
(3), may have been built as a private house for
William, son of the 4th Earl, and wife Elizabeth
Hay. Two rooms on each of the two floors,
servants' quarters in attic reached by a stairtower.
Extensive stables and grooms' accommodation to
south, beside well-appointed **smithy** (4) with
massive chimney and hearth.

George Keith, 5th Earl Marischal (*c*.1553–1623), founder of Marischal College, Aberdeen, succeeded to the title in 1581 and redesigned the fort as a palace. He probably began with the **east range** (5) with apartments for the Countess and library above a larder, brewhouse and bakery. His own wing or pendicle with **Whigs' Vault** (6) below, and spacious parlour and **King's Chamber** above, is a spectacular eyrie on the cliff. The **north range** (7) comprised vaulted stores and gigantic kitchen below with a broad and stately rectangular stairway leading to the first-floor dining hall and great chamber. He continued with the **west range** (8) of seven individual lodgings, each with their own fireplace, front door and two windows. Stately, 35m long **gallery** in floor above, *curiously ceiled with oak and after a very rich form excellently lighted, and at the end of it a stone in the midst of the wall taken out of Hadrian's Wall* (Gordon of Straloch), accessed via the **Silver House** (9), a staircase block to the south with upper storey for keeping valuables. At north end, the long gallery terminated in a withdrawing room with a balcony overlooking the sea.

To protect this gracious living, the **gateway** (10) and **Benholm's Lodging** (11) were constructed on the sharp hillside to the north west. Foundations of the latter are cut into the rock and contain a prison, with more airy apartments stacked above. Outer walls of the lodging are pierced with three tiers of gunloops and through the portcullis one is faced by a firing chamber with four massive gunports, like gouged eye sockets. Like so much militaria in the late 16th century, these are more for show than defence: neatly recessed for glass windows.
Open to the public

Left *Lodgings and gallery.* Top *Smithy.* Middle *Guard room.* Above *Re-used 1645 dormer pediment in King's Chamber.*

In 1716, following his support for the Old Pretender, the 10th Earl Marischal had all his estates confiscated. The York Buildings Company then stripped the castle of whatever remained after the 1652 bombardment. In 1925 Lady Cowdray, advised by William Kelly, organised its consolidation, reroofed the great chamber of the north range, wood panelled the ceiling and added the stone flagged floor based on the pattern at Tolquhon Castle.

KINNEFF AND CATTERLINE
Sea birds, stacked spectacularly in their high-rise nests on the cliffs of Fowlsheugh by Crawton, vastly outnumber the human inhabitants of this coastal windswept parish.

25 **Kinneff Old Parish Church**
Oblong harled box with classical belfry, rebuilt in

Top *Kinneff Old Parish Church.*
Above *Todhead Lighthouse.*

In 1652, when Cromwell's troops were attacking the Scottish Royalists, Charles II ordered the Scottish crown jewels to be sent to Dunnottar for safety. George Ogilvy of Barras, governor of the castle, withstood Cromwell's siege for eight months, and in desperation arranged for the minister of Kinneff's wife, Mrs Grainger, to smuggle the 'Honours' out of the castle to her church. She carried the regalia wrapped in cloths out of the castle and had them concealed under the floor at Kinneff church (colour p.65). Mr Grainger uwrapped them at night once every three months to keep them clean, and concealed them for eight years. In 1660 the crown, sceptre and sword were restored to the nation at a ceremony in Edinburgh Castle. After the Act of Union with England in 1707, the 'Honours of Scotland' remained sealed in a chest until 1818 when Sir Walter Scott, with great excitement and emotion, had its locks prized off and the treasures revealed to the nation.

Joan Eardley, 1921–63, the Glasgow School colourist, lived in South Row, using the houses and the bay as inspiration for her paintings (colour p.67). The passionate impact of her work was a major factor in the decision to conserve the Catterline/Crawton coastline.

South Row, Catterline.

1738 on site of earlier church consecrated in 1242 by Bishop de Bernham of St Andrews. North aisle and staircase added by minister William Mearns, 1876, to designs by J Russell Mackenzie. Retains original seating. Removal of harling, 1981, revealed two original south doors and windows. Bell, 1679, by Pieter Ostens of Rotterdam. Contains 17th-century wall tablets and memorial to Sir George Ogilvy of Barras, Governor of Dunnottar Castle during the siege.

Kinneff Old Manse, 1738
Originally three bays with chimneys at the gable ends, later wings added to north and east forming a courtyard. **Kinneff Castle**, now only a block of masonry on a promontory below the church, probably begun by the de Montforts in the early 13th century, destroyed, 1337. **Castle of Cadden**, another medieval promontory fort, is protected from land by a bank and ditch. A few foundations indicate a small range of buildings. **Whistleberry Castle**, mentioned in the 14th century and inhabited until the mid-17th century, belonged to the Lindsays of Edzell and later to Sir Robert Arbuthnott. Only a fragment of wall face remains. A curtain wall and ditch enclosed the promontory.

26 **Todhead Lighthouse**, 1897, D A Stevenson
On a windy cliff, stumpy white-harled column with corbelled gallery and lantern dome. The drop weights of the original clockwork lighting mechanism required twice the height of the tower in order to operate. Consequently a shaft, as deep as the tower is high, was hewn into the living rock underneath.

27 **Catterline's** former fishermen's cottages cluster on the cliff edge, above the stony crescent bay. **1–10 South Row**, early 19th century, a traditional group of single-storey, whitewashed cottages, each with two windows and central door. Their picturesque isolation, uncluttered by modern in-filling, is legally protected. On the north cliff, rows of beige

harled cottages, modern but in scale. **Trelong Row**, 1984, Nicholson and Jacobson, combines dense housing with good broken roofline.

The **bridge** over Catterline Burn, *c.*1800, has dressed stone voussoirs. The walls of **Catterline Old Burial Ground** enclose a late medieval aumbry and include gatepiers dated 1817. Early medieval incised stone cross-slab and memorial aisle for William Grant Hilton of Tulloch entered beneath a fine classical pediment.

St Philip's Episcopal Church, 1848, Charles Brand Nave, chancel and porch in early Gothic Revival style. Comfortably squat south elevation with windows reaching the eaves.

Mains of Catterline Grove
A steading converted into apartments, 1995, by George Bisset. Original stones have been successfully re-used with recessed pointing to highlight their shape. Rustic-looking windows and wide barn doorways appropriate for the setting.

Fawsyde House, 1865, J Russell Mackenzie H-plan, harled with stone window dressings. Balanced but playful, the windows combine an entertaining variety of gothic and Venetian styles. In garden, **Fawsyde Castle Ruin**, three-storey folly tower with polygonal stairturret. Large rectangular windows and machicolations around the flat roof.

Top *Medieval aumbry, Catterline Old Burial Ground.* Middle *Mains of Catterline Grove.* Above *Fawsyde House.*

Kinneff and Catterline Parish Church, 1843 Former Free Kirk with Norman detailing around windows and entrance.

Sir Robert Arbuthnott regained the lands of Fiddes in the early 16th century. The inscription *I A-H B 1673* on the east side of the house, refers to John Arbuthnott and his wife Helen Burnett.

Castle of Fiddes, 1592
L-plan four-storey tower house, possibly begun 1560s, simply set in a farmyard. Its most charming and dynamic aspect, the re-entrant, is almost perverse in its asymmetry, with a jerky relationship between one component and the next. Principal north/south block has crowstepped gables. Circular staircase in re-entrant extends into main block. Stair topped by an open platform roof with machicolated corbels. Circular tower clasping the south-west angle of main block, capped by square chamber. The other three corners develop into two-storey circular turrets. The date 1592 appears on the carved south-east dormer. Many circular gunloops. Vaulted basement contains kitchen and wine cellar with private stair to first-floor hall. Considerably restored, 1930s; reharled, 1960s.

Castle of Fiddes.

INVERBERVIE

Mercat Cross.

David II, returning from France and being chased by the English, made a forced landing below the cliffs of Bervie Brow. In gratitude for his hospitable welcome he granted Inverbervie the status of royal burgh in 1342, with the rights to hold markets and form a town council. The historic charter was destroyed when the tolbooth and much of the town was burnt on the orders of Regent Moray in 1567. Its status as royal burgh was lost under the Act of Union in 1707. The town's success as a fishing port declined in the late 18th century as the river mouth silted up, and the fishermen moved to Gourdon.

The *Cutty Sark*, launched in 1869, was the fastest tea clipper in its day. It was named after the short shirt worn by the witch Nannie in Robert Burns' *Tam o' Shanter*. Renowned for its ergonomic and elegant design, it is preserved in dry dock at Greenwich, London.

Above Cutty Sark. *Right* Jubilee Bridge *and Old Bervie Bridge.*

Industry sprang up along the river above the bridge: in 1790 the first mechanical mill in Scotland for spinning linen yarn was built and it survived until 1919. Several flax mills using the water power came and went, the sheds below the bridge being a remnant of these.

INVERBERVIE
Mercat Cross, Market Square
On five-step octagonal base, finial dated 1737. The last visible link with the town's illustrious past. **3 & 4 Market Square**, plain, rendered 18th-century houses, **No 3** being the birthplace of Hercules Linton (born 1836), designer of the tea clipper *Cutty Sark*. A memorial to Linton and the ship, 1999, a replacement of the 1969 original by T Scott Sutherland, stands at the south end of Jubilee Bridge. The sculpture is a half-size replica of the ship's figurehead, Nannie holding the tail of Tam's mare.

Jubilee Bridge, 1935
For George V's jubilee, on a stunning curve, seven spans of reinforced concrete, each bay topped by a cast-iron lamp standard. Adjacent **Old Bervie Bridge**, 1799, a single 103ft span with pierced spandrels and vaulted cellars for storing coal and lime in the abutments. The juxtaposition of the two bridges makes a dramatic sight.

Craigview, High Street, 1995,
Kennedy Partnership
Mixed sheltered and private homes in pink and beige pebble-dash with active roofscape in brown pantiles. Scheme respects the scale and colour of adjacent buildings with characterful detailing around doors and windows. Sunny courtyard and gardens designed to provide shelter from the wind.

3a & b David Street, late 18th century
Harled with moulded skewputts. You win some,
you lose some: 1999 restoration salvaged this
well-proportioned house, putting in 'correct'
doors and four-paned sashes, but removed the
distinctive pediment and stringcourse.

Manse, King Street, 1737
Triple pile house, rectangular hoodmoulding
over the windows added to street front, 1918.
Alterations and additions, 1836 and 1877.

Bervie Parish Church, 1837, John Smith
Stern and imposing if somewhat predictable,
making a fine impact from up-river at Arbuthnott.
*The tower is seen to great advantage in all directions and
gives an air of ornament and grandeur to the burgh
which it had not before.* Oblong gothic perpendicular,
with central bell tower, battlemented and
pinnacled. Entrance gates, 1836, John Smith, joined
by a decorative iron lamp arch.

Town House, Church Street, 1720
A restrained and dignified civic building, two
storey, rubble and slate with pedimented central
bay. Council chamber in upper hall. Date stone of
1569 in east gable probably from previous town
house sited in Market Square. Bell survives the
removal of 18th-century belfry.

Former Drill Hall, Victoria Terrace, 1906
Imposing ecclesiastical façade with nook shafts
beside doorway. Single-span laminated timber
braces in roof.

1–12 Castle Terrace, late 19th century
Coherent row of individual three-bay, single-
storey houses with a variety of dormers.
Excellent cast-iron railings in different designs,
fleur-de-lys, urns and balusters, create a united
frontage to the terrace.

Bervie Old Parish Kirk, Kirkburn, 1781
Remains of the west gable, with pointed
unmoulded arches to window and door. Adjacent
to the warm local sandstone cottages at **1-6
Kirkburn**, 1883, **No 8**, 1983, the new manse, a
three-storey, bright yellow Fyfestone intrusion,
abruptly shattering the architectural harmony of
the town centre.

The dramatic curve of Bervie Bay with its
multicoloured pebbles and eroded cliffs to either
end finds no response from the in-filling of the

*From top 3a & b David Street, before
restoration; 3a & b David Street, after
restoration; Bervie Parish Church; Town
House; Former Drill Hall.*

Top *Hallgreen Castle, 1982.*
Above *Hallgreen Castle, 2000.*

Gourdon harbour.

Mary Keith was the infant daughter of the 5th Earl Marischal. Most of her relations are in the family aisle at Dunnottar Church. Her memorial includes bold figure sculptures of a skeleton piercing the Earl and Countess with the darts of death. Many of the Benholm congregation abandoned their parish church in 1790, setting up a Secession church in Waughton Place, Johnshaven (see p.35). The ruction was caused by the minister trying to sing hymns in unison with his flock and no longer *reading the line.*

raised foreshore: the corned beef bowling club, the brown rendered slabs of the sports centre and the straight **Hall Green Road** flanked by uniform white rendered 1980s' bungalows.

28 **Hallgreen Castle**, from 16th century
Substantial and well-preserved remains of a 16th-century L-plan tower with later additions; marriage lintel *WR 1687 HC*, for William Rait. Old south and east fronts, three storeys and attic, small corner turrets. Horizontal figure-of-eight gunloops somewhat like those at Tolquhoun (see *Gordon* in this series). Later wings added to north and west. Restoration by owner Ian MacMillan, 1980s, included reharling and reducing the Victorian south wing to single storey and has produced a fantasy of tiny turrets around a new enclosed western entrance courtyard. Early wing in rubble with ashlar quoins, the courtyard wings faced in ruthless cement harling, Victorian north wing is stugged ashlar. Victorian crenellated bridge crossing picturesque waterfall in grounds. Plaster ceiling with Rait coat of arms, dated 1683, and paintings of landscape and flowers on wainscot, lost following dereliction, 1970s. Now oppressed by encroaching 1980s' housing estates.

GOURDON
An active fishing village. The harbour is flanked by a triple gable stone fish shed, 1896. Houses are mainly workaday single storey with modern roof extensions (colour p.69).

BENHOLM
29 **St Marnoch's Parish Church**, from 1242
At the historic heart of the community, sited on a stunning promontory at the junction of two gorges or 'dens'. The outline of the medieval chancel, consecrated 1242, is preserved in the burial aisle to the east of the present building, erected 1832. Its classic harled and slate exterior conceals a charming original interior arranged

with two tiers of seats facing the pulpit and south windows. Surviving 15th-century **sacrament house** and 1621 wall **memorial** to Mary Keith.

Benholm Manse, 1826
Harl and slate with exposed margins and later ashlar bay window. Ashlar gothic front to 19th-century stables. Unusual **fruit store**, a tiny circular tower with conical slate roof has forestair to the well-ventilated upper storey and internal stair to enclosed cool wine cellar. From here there is a good view of the **bridge** over Castle Burn, dated 1774 with 19th-century parapets. **Kirklea** (former Benholm Schoolhouse) with its central gabled bay has been converted to a private house by the insertion of a second floor. **The Glebe**, a white pebble-dash, picture-window, ranch-style bungalow, complete with red brick paved drive, has been shoe-horned into this historic and scenic settlement, disrupting its quiet integrity.

30 **Benholm Castle**, 15th century
Evocative of past glories struggling to rise again, these ruins loom over a deep ravine. Rectangular four-storey tower crowned with parapet and angle bartizans, later cap-house, rubble with dressed quoins on all corners. Aumbry and carved jambs of the fireplace from the great hall are now in the service wing opposite the tower. Severely restrained Georgian mansion of finely jointed ashlar, in the neoclassical style of John Adam, added to south side and later linked to tower by a curved bay.

The tower was begun by the Lundie family, later owned by the Ogilvies and then the Keiths. It was bought by the Scotts in 1659 who added the mansion later. The new wing was used as a hospital in the Second World War, after which the site became derelict. The east side of the tower collapsed in 1992 pending a decision on consolidation from Historic Scotland, but restoration has painstakingly begun with a new roof and windows for the mansion.

Left *Mary Keith memorial*. Top *Sacrament house*. Middle *Manse fruit store*. Above *Benholm Castle, 1992*.

Right *Mill of Benholm.* Below *Muirton Farmhouse.*

Mill of Benholm, 18th century
L-plan meal mill with attached kiln and external wheel, alterations from 1871. All machinery and water courses complete and working, restored by Kincardine and Deeside District Council, 1982. Featured as Long Rob's Mill in the television adaptation of *Sunset Song.*

Muirton Farmhouse
Substantial late 18th-century house with columned porch and central gablet. Interior gutted and being restored.

JOHNSHAVEN
An active fishing village, specialising in shellfish. Core of low terraces of fisher cottages huddled round narrow wynds. Survival of a genuine coastal fishing industry here means the village retains a more authentic atmosphere and appearance than others like Newtonhill (see p.20) which have succumbed to suburbia. Its considerable charm lies in the wide variety of small-scale houses hugging the hillside. Village is girdled by an unlandscaped caravan park and two-storey social housing which show no awareness of the distinctive traditional scale, layout and materials of the old centre. It thrived in the 18th century, but development was hampered by lack of harbour with decent draught.

Harbour **piers**, 1871 and 1884, include a cobbled slipway leading to **Lifeboat Station**, 1891, with deep eaves and wave-patterned bargeboards. **McBay's** triple-bay fish store has aisles supported by mid-19th-century cast-iron Doric columns. **4 & 10 Dock Street**, typical fisher cottages, single storey, three bay, harled. Many had pantiled roofs, now replaced by slate.

Johnshaven Lifeboat Station.

The great mass of buildings in this place is a congeries of mean cottages, huddled all through one another, without regard to order, plan or accommodation which gave occasion to the remark that Johnshaven had been sown broadcast.
G Robertson, *c.*1800

Hay Cottage, Main Street, mid-19th century
Assertive classical doorpiece with fine pediment on a three-bay, single-storey-and-dormers cottage.

22-23 & 24 Main Street
Recently modernised, losing their original 12-pane sash windows and two additional front

doors; **No 22-23** has Aberdeen bond masonry, **No 24** has swept dormerheads. **Old Manse**, Seaview Terrace, *c.*1850, restrained classical villa with tooled ashlar and corniced door. Original iron railings along the street. Adjacent **Skerry Vore**, triple-gabled converted Free Church from 1840s.

Old Schoolhouse, Seaview Terrace
Comprises schoolroom and house, 1854, and adjacent cottages. Harled with long and short dressings.

The Ship, Castle Street
Three units linked to form the early 19th-century hotel. Squared snecked rubble with stugged dressings. Pilastered doorpiece to central block.

Johnshaven Parish Church, Mid Street, 19th century
Built on two levels, a gable moulding over the entrance to Castle Street; plain lower entrance flanked by twin pointed windows. Gable ends filled with five-light windows with wooden tracery.

13, 14 & 15 Castle Street
Three unusually tall dwellings, two storeys with swept dormers bisecting the roofline on **Nos 14 & 15**. **No 14** has forestair resting on cast-iron stanchion. Once used as a poorhouse.

The significance of houses around **Waughton Place** is now lost with the demolition of the brewery. **Old Brewer's House**, now inscribed 1994; **Old Post Office**, originally late 18th century, restoration has removed original glazing. Opposite, **No 34** has Carmylie stone-flagged roof. **Nos 14-16**, disguised by harling and a variety of modern windows, was originally the Secession Church, dated 1790 on the skewputt (see Benholm Parish Church p.32), now divided into dwellings. **No 21** (Kelowna), *c.*1800, two-storey,

Left *22-24 Main Street.* From top *4 Dock Street; Hay Cottage; Old Schoolhouse; The Ship.*

three-bay tenement originally divided horizontally into two dwellings. Forestair at centre with one front door below and another breaking the eaves with the roof swept over.

Above *Old Brewer's House.*
Right *Lathallan School.*

The estate of Brotherton was bought by James Scott of Logie in 1570. His mansion, demolished 1862, stood on the present terraced lawn and had three wings around a courtyard. Hercules Scott, marrying Anna Moon the daughter of a Liverpool cotton merchant, moved into the new castle in 1868. The house became a school in 1949.

Below *Tomb.* Bottom *Morphie Aisle.*

31 **Lathallan School**, 1866, James Matthews
Vast six-storey baronial former Brotherton Castle, castellated *porte-cochère*, roofline with full complement of crowstepped gables, turrets, caphouse, square and round towers. Lower service wing to south also with towers. Central full-height hall; ornamental plaster ceilings; mahogany, birch and pine furniture in bedrooms designed for the house. Magnificent walled terraced gardens roll down to the sea.

ST CYRUS
Geology divides the settlement into three sharply contrasting areas: the foreshore beneath the towering cliffs, the village clustered around the present church and school, and the uplands which provide good farming and command magnificent views over the sea.

Ecclesgreig
The church on the beach, probably begun by the Culdees and described as an ancient priory in the 12th century. Church rebuilt and dedicated by Bishop William de Bernham of St Andrews, 1242, abandoned 1632. Present roofless box with crowstepped gables is the **Morphie Aisle**, rebuilt by Baron Graham of Morphie in the mid-19th century, with fine coat of arms on the gable. Watch house with chimney.

Fishing station on the beach, in picturesque isolation, used by the inshore salmon fishermen. The **Woodstone Station**, below Nether Woodstone, has a 20ft cube icehouse cut into the cliff, used in the 19th century for packing salmon.

32 **Kirkside House**, from early 17th century
Nestling on a shelf of the slumped cliff, rear
cellar and basement has carved lintel dated 167?
From this evolved the present three-storey rear
wing with moulded architrave around central
door, pronounced rustications with date stone
1764 around central window. South-west front
wing added c.1805, two storeys over older
basement, with a double curved and arched stair
to the Roman Doric columned and pedimented
door, flanked by pilastered Venetian windows.
Bow-fronted wing added to north west by Sir
Robert Lorimer, 1908, with interior woodwork
by Nathaniel Grieve. Final alterations by
William Davidson and Matthew Ochterlony,
c.1928. Owned by the Straton family from
1582–1872. A satisfying and complex house.
Doocot, early 19th century, with ratcourse and
'roans' or cement render over the roof joints.

Kaim of Mathers, c.1420
Built by David de Berkeley following his
murder of the sheriff of Kincardine, after which
he was ordered by James I to live *neither on land
nor water*. The gaunt ruined tower clinging to
its pinnacle above the waves was once 40ft
square and four storeys high.

At the northern foreshore are remains of limekilns
among the spectacular coloured boulders at
Miltonhaven. A band of limestone once formed a
great white sea wall for the busy village protected
behind it. When the lime workers excavated their
own natural dyke, the sea moved in during 1795
and destroyed the village.

On top of the cliff is the **kirkton**, *40 houses
disposed without much regard to neatness and
regularity around the church. The situation is
exceedingly damp and exposed, and appears to
possess no other advantage than that of showing off
the church which has a rather respectable appearance
when seen from a distance* (parish schoolmaster,
1841). The remains of Sir Alexander Straiton's
1632 church now converted into the burial
enclosure for the Porteous family.

Garvock St Cyrus, 1853–4, David Mitchell
Three-bay rectangle with tall lancets, buttressed
and decorated towards the village, plain and
practical towards the sea. A great beacon of a
parish church. Four-stage square tower to north
gable with twin belfry openings, lofty octagonal
spire and weather vane. Interior recast, 1905, A
Marshall Mackenzie.

The first name for this settlement was
Ecclesgreig meaning either 'church of
the rock', 'church of Grig', a Pictish
ruler in the 9th century, or 'church of
Cyrus'. Cyrus was a Roman martyr
who had his brains dashed out while a
baby and became the patron saint of
children in need. His cult was
acknowledged in the *Pictish Chronicle*.
The red sandstone and lava cliffs
combined with the salt flats and sand
dunes to form a National Nature
Reserve, outstanding for its bird life
and carpet of flowers, particularly
beautiful in July.

George Beattie, poet, *his genius forcible
and pathetic*, is buried by Ecclesgreig
churchyard stile. He shot himself in
1823, forsaken by the heiress of Stone of
Morphie Farm, William (her parents
had wanted a son) Gibson.

Kirkside House.

Garvock St Cyrus.

Exasperated by the high-handed
behaviour of Sheriff Melville of
Kincardine, James I exclaimed that he
would not mind if someone *biled the loon
and suppit the bree*. The lairds of
Arbuthnott, Pitarrow, Lauriston and
Mathers threw the sheriff into a
cauldron. *He howled like a wolf in the
warming water, then like a bairn smored in
plague, and his body bloated red as the clay,
till the flesh loosed off from his seething
bones: and the four lairds took their horn
spoons from their belts and supped the broth
that the sheriff made.*
Lewis Grassic Gibbon, *Cloud Howe*

37

School, 1867, William Fettis
Rectangular block with transverse gable wing and ostentatious bellcote over the arched entrance; lancet windows have label stops carved with stern faces and the original dated cast-iron gutters survive. On the new wing are two **relief plaques** of a bird and woman's head in profile, made by Sylvia Stewart in 1990. Altogether attractive use of sandstone detailing.

Manse, from 1797, begun as a two-storey, three-bay house, the gabled wing to the right added 19th century, the porch and back wing before 1850. Extensively repaired, 1871, James Maclaren. **Schoolhouse**, 1780s, two storeys, three bays and fanlight over front door, classically sober and sensible.

Free Church, 1904
Lancet windows and corner buttresses; squat square tower on south side has triple lancet belfry openings, a crenellated parapet and pinnacle on each corner. **Public Hall and Library**, 1912, crowstepped gables and a fine inscription over the door, a plaque surmounted by a winged cherub.

Burnside, 18th century
Dower house for Ecclesgreig House, two storeys, harled with painted margins and moulded skewputts.

Top Relief plaques, St Cyrus School.
Middle Schoolhouse. Above Public Hall
and Library. Right Ecclesgreig House, 1962.

Henry Edmund Goodridge, 1797–1864, son of James Goodridge, the major builder of Bath, initially worked in Greek revival style, but also designed several gothic revival churches.

Ian Begg, was a partner with Robert Hurd, 1963–83; from 1985 in partnership with Raymond Muszynski. Best known for his substantial historical revivals, the Scandic Crown Hotel (see *Edinburgh* in this series), and the St Mungo Museum, Glasgow, built in random rubble over a steel frame.

33 **Ecclesgreig House**, 1844,
Henry Edmund Goodridge
Gaunt shell towering above the village, built for F G Forsyth-Grant; soon afterwards elaborated by David Mitchell. This Jacobean dream palace, originally called Mount Cyrus, incorporates some earlier elements: on the south-east front an inscription of 1635 is inserted and there are old

rubble walls at the back of the house. The rest is crisply detailed sandstone ashlar. Symmetrical south-east front has a three-storey central bay with crowstepped gable flanked by turrets. Two pairs of bays either side have patterned gables, the façade ending in two more turrets. North-east entrance front has a mighty tower rising above the *porte-cochère*. Tower to south west changes from square to circular and is topped by a tall slender spire. Derelict garden laid out with elegant balustrades and parterres. Currently used as a farm store.

The situation, on the brink of a perpendicular precipice, overhanging a deep wooded ravine, is exceedingly romantic, and the walks, approaches, bridges and plantations render this place one of the most delightful residences in the county.
New Statistical Account, 1845

Below *Lauriston Castle, 1890.*
Bottom *Lauriston Castle, 1993.*

RCAHMS

34 **Lauriston Castle**, from 14th century
Facing a splendid prospect over the sea, a curious cluster of disparate buildings in rubble, white harling and brown ashlar. The 14th-century polygonal courtyard castle was extended in the 17th century to L-plan tower house. On the west side, one of the original square corner towers rises six storeys out of the living rock above a deep gorge. Its original height is marked by corbels, campanile extension added in Victorian times. L-plan tower house was in turn absorbed into the back of a pedimented three-storey Georgian country house, 1765 and 1789. Onto the east of this somewhat severe but dignified mansion, a further wing of two storeys and six bays, in ashlar with balustraded parapet, was added in the 19th century for Alexander Porteous. After its use as barracks in the Second World War and subsequent neglect, part of the tower house collapsed into the Den and the Georgian mansion was demolished. Ian Begg replaced this derelict part of the site for William Newlands in 1994 with a totally new castle design, including a great hall and wide wheel staircase, doocot with cap-house and an extended curtain-wall pierced with viewing windows over the Den. The result is a picturesque

W Newlands

In 1243 the first Lauriston Castle belonged to the Stirling family of Glenesk and was demolished in 1336 by the Regent Sir Andrew Moray. Shortly afterwards, the Straitons built the existing old corner tower. From 1695 to 1793 the family of James Falconer of Phesdo owned the castle. Mr Brand, bank manager from Montrose, owned the house in the late 18th century. Alexander Porteous, promoter of the Montrose and Bervie Railway Company bought it in 1849 and was responsible for the landscaping. He was the first merchant to introduce jute from Calcutta to Dundee. After his son failed to sell the property in 1931, it fell into almost total decay except for the 19th-century wing and was only rescued by William Newlands in the 1980s.

Bridgeton.

and practical home, adding vitality to a splendid location, and extending the 500-year sequence of styles (colour p.70). Below, a dramatic garden tumbles with terraces and bridges into the gorge.

Quarryfield
Former Lauriston Home Farm has fine mid-19th-century castellated steading with square doocot tower over the central bay. **East Mathers Steading**, from early 19th century, attempts to create a classical design with three symmetrical pavilions, harled with painted margins, but is in poor condition.

Geddes

35 **Bridgeton**, 1841
An ambitious baronial creation. Circular turrets, crowstepped gables and a magnificent centrepiece over the entrance: the framing of the door and heraldic plaque extends around the first-floor window. The regrettable loss of its original harling has left the dark rubble walls predominating over the crisp detail.

Denfinella Bridge, *c.*1817
Carries the A92 north from the village over a precipitous gorge. Rustic Piranesian masonry on south face is worth getting out of the car to see.

36 **Lower North Water Bridge**, 1770–5
Has an inscription identifying John Smeaton, John Adams and Andrew Barrie of Montrose as the architects and engineers. Seven segmental river arches with cutwaters, keyblocked circles in spandrels flanking the central arch. The disused **Bervie Branch Railway Viaduct**, 1861–5, Blyth and Blyth Engineers, with bull-faced masonry piers, is beside the road bridge. The two bridges make an impressive combination, linking Kincardine with Angus.

Lower North Water Bridge and Bervie Branch Railway Viaduct.

Geddes

The Marykirk road passes the megalithic **Stone of Morphie**, a mighty sentinel *c.*2500–1500 BC.

Mill of Morphie House, late 18th century
Rubble built with moulded skewputts and a fine
stone-slated roof. Substantial remains of mill
equipment lie between the house and river.

Forebank House.

During the agricultural improvements
of the mid-18th century, *the cow was
expelled from the family seat and compelled
to walk, with indignant usage, into a
separate apartment by a different entry. The
dunghill still kept immemorial possession of
its station by the house door.*
George Robertson, early 1800s

37 **Forebank House**, 1757
The distinguished dower house to Inglismaldie
Castle (see p.44), hence its superior design and
quality. Two-storey, five-window façade with
basement and attic, architraved doorpiece has
cornice and fanlight. Gables have oval windows
on first floor lighting a central spinal corridor and
twin bull's-eye windows for the attic (colour p.65).

MARYKIRK
Formerly Aberluthnott, the village perches on a
low ridge above the flood plain of the North Esk.
The parish is distinguished by fertile sheltered
land and some magnificent, prosperous farms.

Below *North Esk House.* Middle
Marykirk Hotel. Bottom *Adams Building.*

North Esk House, *c.*1800, the old manse, has an
arched and keyblocked doorpiece with fanlight.
North of the church is the **Market Cross** base,
two rectangular blocks supporting the remains of
an octagonal shaft, possibly 17th century.

Marykirk Hotel, 18th century
Two-storey, three-window harled inn; wing with
cantilevered veranda added 19th century, stables
converted to bar.

The **High Street** has lost some of its character due
to pebble-dash and modern windows on one side
and a ribbon of bungalows on the riverside. Only
No 2, Mary Mill Cottage, retains its stone-flagged
roof. **Adams Building** remains a distinctive late
18th-century structure, with central gablet,
moulded skewputts and doorpiece carved with
Masonic signs.

41

Old Kirkyard

Raised well above natural ground level by centuries of burials, could be even older than the first recorded church of 1242. Nothing survives except its aisles. To the north, the ivy-covered vault of the Barclays of Balmakewan, the Barclay arms lurking beneath the foliage, and to the south the **Thornton Aisle** with aumbry, font and a Strachan inscription: *A 1615 S*. Inside, memorial to *the fragrant memory* of Dame Elizabeth Forbes from 1661, in fine sculptured marble. Aisle sadly roofless, locked and full of debris. Adjacent, new church of **St Mary Aberluthnott**, 1806, alterations James Matthews, 1893. Well-lit hall of three bays with balcony at the west end. The roof trusses form two impressive pointed arches and all the pews are stripped to their natural colour. Gothic Revival wooden font.

The **lodges** to Kirktonhill House are set between fine neoclassical gates and railings. The recent extensions are suited in scale and colour to their early 19th-century ashlar core.

Top *Font, St Mary Aberluthnott*. Above *Memorial to Dame Elizabeth Forbes*. Right *Kirktonhill House, 1837, by Dr Walter Kinnear*. Below *Kirktonhill Tower*.

38 **Kirktonhill House**, 1799

Rebuilt for the Taylor family of Montrose whose fortune came from sugar estates in Jamaica. Austere U-plan house with three-storey front, two bays on each side of a central bow. It declined after being requisitioned during the Second World War, the front of the house finally demolished in the 1960s. Servants' and nursery wings which projected from the back are now two independent houses, with a garage on the site of the Georgian mansion. Two massive walled gardens, one partly brick and one stone still survive, together with **Kirktonhill Tower**, a stone folly of two circular storeys projecting from an octagonal base.

Left *Balmanno House.* Below *Marykirk Bridge.*

39 Balmanno House, *c.*1790

Generously proportioned five-bay dower house for Kirktonhill in coursed rubble with finely carved architrave doorpiece. Impressive setting with an extensive view to the hills, mature trees, walled garden and coach house. Equivalent to Forebank, St Cyrus (see p.41), a fine example of the middling-sized house which is quite rare in this area.

Towards the river are **Spear Mill**, early 18th century, with fine stone ashlar and a moulded stringcourse adjacent to the (missing) wheel; and **Mary Mill**, early 19th century, which retains its cast-iron wheel frame.

Upper North Water Bridge.

Marykirk Bridge, 1811–14, Robert Stevenson Four segmental arches with recessed circular panels in the spandrels and fine ashlar cutwaters. The nearby railway bridge is made with straight cast- and wrought-iron sections. Further upstream, formerly carrying the Aberdeen/Dundee highway, **Upper North Water Bridge**, 16th century, repaired 1809, widened, 1841, by John Gibb. Three arches with square ribs, decayed heraldic plaque on the west side and wrought-iron parapet.

Myreside Farmhouse, *c.*1820

Has unusual original windows with lying-pane glazing. **Marykirk School and Schoolhouse** moved from the village in 1826, but the first record of the present building is 1842. The south-west front shows the generous three-bay schoolhouse attached to school wing on the right. The latter was one tall storey until a recent fire when it was rebuilt with two floors.

Myreside Farmhouse.

40 Hatton Mains House, from late 17th century

Modest but peacefully prosperous house and farm. U-plan, two-storey, harled central block,

43

Hatton Mains House.

date stone on right wing, 1746, now covered by harling, front porch c.1830. Similar structure to Auchlunies, Maryculter (see p.79). Graffiti under the excellent woodgrained panelling in study of left wing gives the date 1742 and initials RM and PM of the Montgomery family, owners until 1920 when it was sold to the Henry family. It retains a gentle, lived-in family atmosphere. The mature 18th-century policies have an oval walled garden, ashlar-faced towards the house, **stables** and **coach house**. Derelict **doocot**, lean-to single chamber, crowstepped with ratcourse at the back.

Right *Balmakewan House, 1789, by Robert and John Adam.* Below *Balmakewan House.*

41 **Balmakewan House**, c.1825

Robert and John Adam's design for Thomas Gillies, 1789, was unbuilt. Present mansion severely classical, with the pretensions of a smart town house in Montrose. Warm brown ashlar, two storeys with a basement sunk in the area. Doric-columned doorpiece on advanced central bay. Spacious interior with central top-lit hall, much altered in the later 19th century when the two-bay rear extension was added. *It stands on rising ground and is a neat and commodious structure surrounded and sheltered by thriving and highly ornamental plantations* (*New Statistical Account*, 1842). Beyond the farm, **twin doocots**, c.1800, with perky tea-caddy roofs. Good modern wrought-iron gate.

Doocot, Balmakewan House.

Door panel, Inglismaldie.

42 **Inglismaldie**, from late 16th century

The astonishingly red sandstone of the main block gleams like a flaming ruby in the sunset, vibrating against the copper beeches of the sheltering parkland. With three storeys and attic, it dominates the later wings added to three sides. Three turrets to main front, one at each corner and the third unusually placed at the wallhead, off-centre and flanking the gable. Elaborate label-corbels support the turrets, the same design repeated on broken stringcourse at second-floor level. Fine modern doorway with **heraldic panel**; original entrance, now concealed externally by west wing, led into splendid stone vaulted

RCAHMS

Inglismaldie, pre 1880.

turnpike staircase embellished with double shot holes. Medieval chapel, the original Eccles Maldie, replaced by 19th-century service wing, but its rare mid-16th-century woodwork of flamboyant tracery and heads in roundels was re-used on doors and a mantelpiece in the house.

Austere and barrack-like wing, three storeys and attic with north-west angle turret added to west in late 17th century. Mid-18th-century two-storey south-east wing with hipped roof. This state is shown in the pre-1880s' photograph. James Matthews replaced tall west block after fire, 1882, with two-storey wing in warm brown sandstone with carved pediment dormers. Turret tops on old block reconstructed (higher than original); south-east wing reroofed with crowstepped gables; subsequent alterations to south-east wing, circular south-west tower added, and elaborate service accommodation (colour p.66).

Extensive **walled garden** has been breached in several places to provide a sheltered location for modern 'executive' homes. The stable block is converted to dwellings and the 18th-century **doocot**, with nest boxes for 1,520 birds, is roofless.

RAF Edzell looks like a ghost town since it was abandoned in 1997 after 57 years as an air base and latterly as an early-warning radar station for the Americans. The druidical circle of radar antennae has been dismantled, the huge hangars are empty and the still-spruce married quarters have grass up to their windows. Now being converted to storage and local housing.

Luthermuir

Distinguished from the other scattered settlements in Marykirk by its two neat rows of terraced cottages tucked beside each other on **Main Street**. Each single-storey house has two small windows and a door opening straight onto the road. It was a village for hand-loom linen weavers, flourishing between 1800 and 1840. **Chapel**, 1822, a simple box with two lancet diamond-pane windows and

The church lands of St Maldie were eventually acquired in 1635 by Sir John Carnegie, Sheriff of Forfar, Earl of Northesk. In 1693 David Falconer of Haulkerton (see Fordoun p.54) acquired the castle and his descendants became the Earls of Kintore. A major sale of the castle contents took place in 1925, dispersing relics of the church, after which it reverted to a relation of the Falconer line. In 1959 the castle was in poor condition and it was proposed to use it as a chicken house, but the McBay family, shellfish merchants from Johnshaven, rescued it and restored the roof. It remains in private ownership as a family home.

Below *Doocot, Inglismaldie.* Middle *Chapel, RAF Edzell.* Bottom *Main Street, Luthermuir.*

Geddes

Geddes

Geddes

45

James Macrae belonged to the Berean sect which believed in the absolute truth of the Scriptures. The parishioners were determined to obtain the minister of their choice and petitioned the king that they would fight for His Majesty till their boots were full of blood upon getting their minister ... and if they are frustrated, unforseen disturbances may take place, the peace and quiet of families broken up in flame and riot and disorder, the one against the other. An extreme fondness for religious disputation seemed to constitute a part of the inhabitants' nature (minister, 1793).

wrought-iron bellcote on the gable. **Muirton House**, mid-19th-century former manse, two storeys, three windows and harling. The curved staircase has delicate cast-iron railings. Near Luther Mains, three carved stones from **Caldhame Castle** are set into the wall of a shed, including date stone (16)71 and Barclay coat of arms.

Sauchieburn Berean Chapel, 1773
Now a barn, it marks the serious religious free spirit in this area, built in protest against the choice of minister at Fettercairn. The preferred nominee, James Macrae, was installed at Sauchieburn and set up the first Sunday School in Scotland in a separate room of his simple church.

Pitgarvie Farm
Resplendent with lime avenue, planted 1988, and decorative ironwork sign. **Dowrieburn Pig Farm** illustrates 21st-century agribusiness, with buildings not unlike some at RAF Edzell and ominous smoke stacks.

Geddes

Geddes

RCAHMS

Thornton Castle originally belonged to the Thorntons of that Ilk but was acquired by marriage in 1309 by the Strachan family who held it until the 17th century. Their arms are on the heraldic panel on the north-east tower. It was later the home of Lord Gardenstone, the creator of Laurencekirk (see p.52). In the early 19th century it was acquired by the Crombies, owners of Phesdo, who restored and enlarged the house. The fourth Alexander Crombie and his brother Francis introduced the game of rugby to Scotland, having learnt it at school in Durham in 1852–3. Sir Thomas Thornton, a lawyer and Town Clerk of Dundee, bought back his family estate in 1893, and it remains as the family home of the Thornton-Kemsleys to this day.

43 **Thornton Castle**, from 14th century
Two vigorous and vertical elements, the eastern round tower and L-plan tower house of 1531, are somewhat tamed and domesticated by the 16th-century linking north wing. The base of the round tower, constructed with massive whinstone boulders, is a relic from an earlier complex which extended over the present forecourt. The elaborate chequered bank of corbels supporting the parapet and open angle turrets is the most striking feature of the main tower, three storeys high, topped by two crowstepped cap-houses and weather vane dated 1680.

Barrel-vaulted north wing has massive kitchen fireplace which may be earlier than 1662 date stone. Remodelling, 1822, included the addition of the south (garden) wing, parallel to the north wing onto which parapets were added. Similar chimneyheads by John Smith at Phesdo, also owned by Crombie (see p.57), suggest Smith also worked at Thornton.

In the 1890s Sir Thomas Thornton replaced the original doorway and turnpike in the re-entrant with the formal entrance hall and sweeping staircase lit by stained glass which were pushed through the north wing and tower base. He also added the flat-roofed billiard room to west.

Early 20th-century, state-of-the-art bathroom and toilet, with wall-to-wall Doulton tiles and brass/mahogany ablution centre. House formerly harled in white.

The sporting Crombies built a splendid wood-panelled **cricket pavilion** for the estate and constructed the stable block with its fine ogee-cupola **clocktower**.

FETTERCAIRN

The compact rosy square in the centre announces that this tiny village was once a burgh of barony from 1604, holding a weekly market. The lower part of the **Mercat Cross** may be a relic, transported from the former county town of Kincardine. On the shaft is a groove marking the statutory length of the 'ell' (37½ inches) while the capital, made in 1670, has a sundial and the arms of John, 1st Earl of Middleton, owner of Fettercairn.

Behind the Victorian panelling in the great hall is a wall painting of Dame Elizabeth Forbes (died 1661), whose other memorial is in the Thornton aisle, Marykirk church (see p.42).

Stable clock, Thornton Castle.

Opposite above *Sauchieburn Berean Chapel;* below *Pitgarvie Farm;* right *Thornton Castle.*

Left *The Square, north-west side.* Below *Village shop.* Bottom *Mercat Cross.*

On the north-west side of **The Square**, late 18th-century house with forestair and 20th-century swept dormers; **No 3** has good vernacular 19th-century porch. **Village shop** is part of a row with canted bays at each end. **Kirkhill Farm Houses** have two architraved doorpieces with inset pilasters. Baronial **Public Hall**, 1890, John Milne of St Andrews. Gothic memorial fountain to Sir John S Forbes, 1869, David Bryce architect, John Rhind sculptor (colour p.67). Neat black-and-white **Fettercairn Distillery**, rebuilt after a fire in 1889 (colour p.66).

Queen Victoria and Prince Albert, with their daughter Alice and her husband Prince Louis of Hesse, had ridden for 40 miles over Mount Keen, arriving in the dark at the Ramsay Arms Hotel. They ate supper incognito and went for a stroll in the village. On hearing a band strike up, they were afraid they had been recognised but were informed by a child that the band regularly paraded up the village street. *How odd!* noted the queen in her journal. Another guest was told the hotel was fully booked by a wedding party from Aberdeen. When the group left next morning, a few villagers came out to wave. The queen continued her journey, walking her pony most of the way up Cairn o' Mount.

Royal Arch, 1864, John Milne
A competition design of Rhenish Romanesque, selected by the queen, built to commemorate a clandestine visit by Queen Victoria in 1861. **Ramsay Arms Hotel**, redeveloped 1896–7, Thomas Martin Cappon and Harry East, with fine Arts & Crafts staircase and porch. Its east façade presents a bold block with asymmetrical windows and canted chimney.

Parish Church, 1804
Its location on a conical mound above a stream is typical of the early church. The graveyard has some good 17th- /18th-century tombstones, including one of 1737 depicting the Temptation with Adam in breeches. **Tower**, 1838, John Henderson; interior remodelled 1926, G P K Young.

44 **Balbegno**, from 16th century
Early 16th-century L-plan tower, extended in 1569 with eight new rooms and a stair in the re-entrant, giving the opportunity to gut the old tower and insert an overscaled vaulted hall. Old tower's parapet removed, and entire structure subordinated to the new tower of chambers. Lively roofline of crowsteps and cap-house contains numerous sculptured plaques including heads in roundels, perhaps related to the early 17th-century carvings at Edzell.

The two-bay, rib-vaulted hall, similar to Towie Barclay (see *Banff & Buchan* in this series), has springers for the vault carved as grotesque heads. Building's design also related to Gight, Craigston and Delgatie (see *Banff & Buchan* in this series). Vault extensively covered in heraldic paintings related to the ruling families of Scotland. Tower now uninhabited.

John Wood extended Balbegno in 1569. His family were hereditary constables of Kincardine Castle. The painted ceiling represents the arms of

Top Royal Arch. *Above* Parish Church. *Right* Balbegno.

the earls who removed the Regent Morton in 1581, the scheme representing the political allegiance and ambitions of Andrew Wood and his wife Helen Stewart. Like the heraldic ceiling of St Machar's Cathedral, 1522 (see *Aberdeen* in this series), this rare survivor preserves a crucial moment in Scottish history.

The pleasant 18th-century **farmhouse**, added by the Ogilvy family as a more practical domestic wing, contains some older masonry to rear. Its stately setting includes a terraced **garden** and doocot.

45 The Burn, 1791

Memorable for its outstanding location beside the North Esk gorge, a landscape considerably tamed and sculpted by the stands of beech trees planted by Lord Adam Gordon *c.*1800. Built for Lord Gordon, possibly by James Playfair (compare staircase of Melville Castle, see *Midlothian* in this series). An honest, square Georgian box with pediment over the east front and crisp ashlar details, on much older site. The fine double-height hall, with delicate plastered ceiling and good entrance door, is original, as is the classic **stable yard** and clocktower. The coal baron George Herbert Russell transformed the place in 1933, gutting all the rooms except the hall, adding bays to the south front, redesigning the roof and adding the extensive service wing to the west. Now used as a study centre for university students.

Left *Torwood Cottage.* Top *Lunette in garden wall, Balbegno.* Middle *The Burn.* Above *Stables.*

Gannochy Bridge, 1792, widened by Lord Adam Gordon in 1796, leaps across the gorge (colour p.68).

Torwood Cottage, early 19th century
Delicate and refined neoclassical house, on a comfortably domestic scale. Bow front has four

James Playfair, 1755–94, was the fourth son of the Revd James Playfair, minister for Liff and Benvie in Angus. Nothing is known about James' early life or training as an architect, but by 1783 he was established in London, with an office in Bloomsbury, and began to exhibit regularly in the Royal Academy. His practice was largely in Scotland, where he secured Henry Dundas as a patron. Playfair's predilection for refined neoclassical simplicity is most manifest in the remarkable mausoleum at Methven and at Cairness House (see *Perth & Kinross* and *Banff & Buchan* in this series). His career ended prematurely by his death at the age of 39 through, according to Joseph Farrington, *a broken heart in consequence of the death of his eldest boy.*
A Biographical Dictionary of British Architects, 1600-1840

49

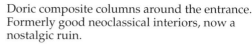

Doric composite columns around the entrance. Formerly good neoclassical interiors, now a nostalgic ruin.

Arnhall House, mid-18th century
Finely proportioned, two storeys with later canted dormers and steep pitched roof, attic windows in gable end. Harled and whitewashed with margins. Modern open porch, good walled garden. On the site of 16th-century Aurinhall House, with date stone of 1622 above mantelpiece.

Above Arnhall House. Right William Burn's façade, Fettercairn House.

Garden view, Fettercairn House.

William Burn, 1789–1870, trained in Robert Smirke's office and was in partnership with David Bryce, 1841–50. By 1840 he had designed or altered over 90 country houses. His early style reflected that of Smirke, in uncompromising Greek revival (Camperdown House, 1821; Edinburgh Academy, 1822–4), while the New Club, Edinburgh, 1834, was Italian palazzo style. His country houses were bold essays in gothic, Tudor, Jacobean and classical, high baroque at Harlaxton, finally reaching Scottish Baronial. *His work is more remarkable for its quantity than its quality* (H M Colvin).

Williamina Forbes of Fettercairn, who rejected Sir Walter Scott as a suitor, married William Forbes, executor to James Boswell. Boswell's papers, which included three journals and over 1,000 letters, some from Samuel Johnson, lay forgotten in some chests until their discovery in 1930, when they were sold to America.

46 **Fettercairn House**, from 1670
Long, low house with two very different personalities: the bombastic, overblown Jacobethan front, and the more muted, genteel 17th-century rear. The original block, now facing the garden, was designed for John Earl Middleton in 1670, recognisable by its rubble finish, with two storeys, attic and rectangular stair house. The five symmetrical bays are reminiscent of the 1619 wing at Drum (see p.84). Additional 17th-century bays to west end in two ogee-roofed turrets.

North-west entrance wing was added in 1826–9 by William Burn for Sir John Stuart Forbes, a wealthy Edinburgh banker, robbing the fine old house of its dignity and scale with his grandiose extension. In its own right however, this is a very early and fine example of Jacobean revival. Single storey over basement, characterised by cavernous mullion and transom windows; to counter their horizontality, they are set against curled gables, probably copied from Montacute, Somerset. The entrance has a rectangular oriel above and is tightly flanked by polygonal buttresses, deriving from Burghley House, Lincolnshire. Inside, high ribbed vault entrance hall and drawing room with elaborate caryatid fireplace. East addition at right angles to house, 1877, Wardrop and Reid. Comfortable old library has a frieze by Robert Lorimer, 1898.

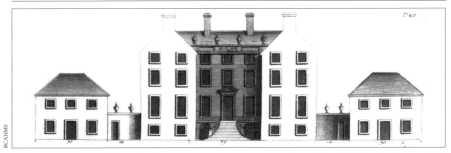

RCAHMS

47 Fasque, 1809, possibly John Paterson
Design by William Adam of four-storey classical
mansion with two pavilions unexecuted. Majestic
castellated mansion in muted brown sandstone for
Sir Alexander Ramsay of Balmain. Symmetrical
main block has central canted bay with Doric
portico, added 1829 for Sir John Gladstone. Lateral
wings flanked by angle turrets create a varied,
stepped façade (colour p.71). Outstanding features
of the house are the sweeping double top-lit
staircase, Corinthian hall at the upper level and
warren of servants' quarters. Stairs are cantilevered
and the original double glazing is engraved.

Since Sir John Gladstone bought the estate in
1829, the minutiae of domestic paraphernalia have
simply accumulated and now present a unique
insight into the daily life of a Victorian country
household. He greatly improved the housing of his
tenants, set up a school and added the tower to
Fettercairn church. Serious landscaping and tree
planting began at Fasque in the 1730s and the
existing stands of beech and rhododendron show
continuing interest of the Gladstones. Delightful
mid-19th-century **pavilion** allows refined garden
enthusiasts to survey the double walled garden.
Open to the public in summer

St Andrew's Episcopal Church, 1847,
John Henderson
In the trees beside Fasque, in the Early English
style, for Sir John Gladstone. New chancel added,
1869. Memorials and glass mainly for the
Gladstone family.

The site of the great royal castle and county town
48 of Kincardine is now only a dusty lane and a
mound covered in trees, haunted by silent feet and
empty house plots (colour p.67). The castle was
being used by Kenneth III at the time of his murder
in 994. The present ruins are of a 13th-century
curtain-wall castle, with two huge round perimeter
towers, one protecting the gateway over a moat.
The major domestic range was on the east side.

*Fasque House, William Adam's unexecuted
design from* Vitruvius Scoticus.

Faskie, the predecessor of Fasque: *There
are a good many apartments in it, especially
the dining room and library. Just by the west
end there is a den or hollow with a Chinese
bridge thrown over it, and a small brook at the
bottom. It is planted and laid out in
serpentine walks.*
Francis Douglas, *East Coast of Scotland*,
1780

Sir John Gladstone, 1764–1851, was a
wealthy Liverpool grain merchant and
MP. His youngest son was William Ewart
Gladstone, 1809–98, Britain's longest-
serving prime minister. He enjoyed
growing up here, and the extensive
library, with many gifts from grateful
admirers, is his collection.

Geddes

Garden pavilion, Fasque.

Under William the Lion, 1143–1214, the
Carnegies were installed as hereditary
constables of the castle and William
became the first Falconer, later Earls of
Kintore and owner of Haulkerton. John
Balliol signed his abdication in favour of
Edward I in the hall of **Kincardine
Castle** in 1296. Mary, Queen of Scots
was the last ruler to visit the castle and
in 1531 it was made *principal and capital
burgh of the county*. By 1607 the seat of
the county court had transferred to
Stonehaven. The castle was finally
dismantled by John Middleton in 1646.

High Street, looking south.

Lord Gardenstone, 1721–93, was a judge and Lord of Session who lived at Thornton Castle (see p.46). In addition to establishing the weaving industry in Laurencekirk, he helped the ingenious snuff-box maker Charles Stiven to set up a business in the town. Gardenstone wrote that he never relished anything so much *as the pleasure arising from the progress of my village.* According to Boswell he was as proud of his creation *as if he had founded Thebes.* Gardenstone's best friend was a pig who slept with his lordship, covered by his breeches when it grew too big for the bed, and who accompanied him up the street for tours of inspection. Gardenstone also knew Dr Johnson, James Beattie and Robert Burns.

Laurencekirk after 1781 *consists of a straight street composed chiefly of houses of one storey, some of them still built of clay and covered with thatch, and mean enough in appearance but intermixed with several two stories and in a genteel style.*
G Robertson, *c.*1800

Below *60 High Street.* Middle *Parish Kirk.* Bottom *Garvocklea.*

LAURENCEKIRK
Retains the homogeneous aspect of a planned town, sprouting out of a fertile agricultural landscape. While the house fronts press close to the pavement of the main street, their back gardens stretch out into fields. This is because the town was founded between 1764 and 1779 (when it became a burgh of barony) by Francis, Lord Gardenstone, as a centre for the Mearns hand-loom weaving of linen, and its house plots were to extend 830yds on each side of the highway, hence 'the lang toon'. At its peak in the 1830s, 147 weavers worked in the town, but development here came to a halt when power mills in the cities took over.

Cottages along the main street are mostly one or one-and-a-half storeys high, with a small window on each side of the front door. **60 High Street** has a Venetian window on the front gable, **No 81** has a good Doric portal.

Parish Kirk, 1804, enlarged 1819
Gothic, rubble and slate; **bell tower**, 1895, James Matthews and A Marshall Mackenzie. Its site, by a steep bank above the burn, may be the original Kirkton of Conveth mentioned in medieval charters. **Episcopal Church**, 1873, Alexander Ross, a well-proportioned box with high roof and low eaves. **Frogfield**, Station Road, one of the few elegant mansions, has a front wing of 1832, with Doric porch and later wing to rear with a large perpendicular window. **Garvocklea** (formerly The Villa), built as a playful hunting lodge in the early 19th century, combines a Doric portal with a Venetian window and crenellations around the wallhead. Much extended at the back.

Laurencekirk was an important coaching halt on the Aberdeen/Dundee road. The **Gardenstone Arms Inn** (former Boar's Head Inn), 1770s, two storey, harled and slated, with two later wings

stretching forward to form a courtyard. Lintel over the front door is dated 1638 but may be re-used; date stones on the wings, now harled over, are inscribed 1774 and 1778.

Laurence's Coach House Hotel, Alma Place, late 18th century
Originally three bays, but extended on both sides to make a long frontage, with pend, 12-pane sashes and canted dormers. **Royal Hotel**, Conveth Place, stugged ashlar, castellated portal and 1894 date stone on east wing.

The railway regenerated Laurencekirk for a while as a market town with an important **cattle market** by the (partially demolished) station. It is only now expanding as a dormitory town for Aberdeen and Montrose, with local industry in sheds focused on farm machinery maintenance. The new **Primary School**, 1996, Joe Humphrey for Grampian Regional Council, reiterates the long, low, grey look of the town, covering the many open-plan teaching areas with a wide sweeping roof.

Top and above *Gardenstone Arms Inn*. Left *Johnston Lodge*.

Lord Gardenstone furnished the inn with a public library, *a very neat assortment of amusing books.* Dr Johnson visited it in 1773 when Boswell recommended the *collection of books that travellers might have entertainment for the mind as well as the body.* The Doctor praised the design of the north end of the building (a tiny classical aedicule, now demolished) but wished there had been *more books and better chosen.* Robert Burns, a guest in 1787, showed more appreciation for the community: *Lie at Laurence Kirk – album – library – Mrs ... a jolly frank, sensible love-inspiring widow.* The painted pub sign is of Lord Gardenstone clutching his pig.

49 **Johnston Lodge**, *c.*1805
For James Farquhar MP, takes elegant advantage of its site on the slope above Laurencekirk. A stone in one of the older rear wings is inscribed *DB 1642 ED*, while the front is a Regency mansion with three-window bow flanked by two bays on each side, and Doric entrance portico on adjacent façade. Bellcote at rear; additions, 1934. In grounds, **chalybeate spring**, possibly late 18th century, in a niche flanked by fluted and panelled pilasters, topped by a pediment with carved face finials. **Johnston Lodge Mains Farmhouse**, 18th century, two storey, newly harled and slated, has a re-used carved dormer pediment embedded in the front wall. Picturesque **Gardener's Cottage** and **West Lodge**, early 19th century, single storey, Tudor gothic, with octagonal ended bays; Gardener's

Cattle market.

The Falconers were the hereditary keepers of royal falcons at Kincardine Castle, with their seat at Haulkerton. Their descendants became the Earls of Kintore, 1677.

Mill of Conveth.

Geddes

William Greig's tomb.

RCAHMS

The Hill of Garvock was the site of the notorious murder of the unpopular Sheriff of Kincardine in 1420 (see St Cyrus, p.37). The hill provided a retreat for Laurencekirk's great intellectual James Beattie, 1735–1803. His *Essay on Truth*, 1771, defended Christianity against the attacks of David Hume.

St Palladius was a 5th-century Irish missionary. His life is obscure but he may have worked in Wicklow before settling in the Mearns, or perhaps his relics were brought to Fordoun. He was sent to Ireland, campaigning against the Pelagian heresy, by Pope Celestine I, 422–32.

Cottage retaining its original gothic glazing, encircling veranda supported by tree trunks.

Castle of Haulkerton is lost but carved stones survive on **Mains of Haulkerton** barn, one a corbel of a head with a hat; there is a stone inscribed *LAF 1648*, referring to the Falconer family.

Mill of Conveth, 18th century
Substantial mill which processed the acres of grain in the vicinity. Although the machinery is dismantled, the interior floors are intact, as is the pyramid-topped kiln.

GARVOCK
Garvock Parish Church, 1778, on the site of a much older building, beside a steep stream bank. Distinctive birdcage bellcote with Renaissance balusters; 17th-century **tomb** of William Greig, illustrating all his tools. **Garvock School**, 1865, and old **Manse**, 1866, both by William Henderson; manse has gaunt gothic bays with later extensions, facing a vast view to the sea.

FORDOUN
Fordoun is a parish of contrasts, where the wide, open red prairies of the Mearns bump into steep and narrow wooded glens. It developed around the relics of St Palladius, for which Bishop Schevez of St Andrews (1479–97) donated a silver shrine.

50 **St Palladius' Chapel**, *c*.16th century
Disappointing rectangular roofless ruin, with round-arched tomb recess, simple late medieval piscina and aumbry. Deep burial vault beneath the floor. Site typical of the early church, at the top of a steep bank above the living water of the Luther. Ancient holy well in manse garden.

Parish Church, 1827–9
Typical of John Smith, in neo-perpendicular style. Conspicuous west tower, originally like that at Footdee (See *Aberdeen* in this series), suffers from the loss of its extended pinnacles and open parapet (colour p.68). Pictish stone with symbols and hunting scene found buried in the main church, now in the vestibule. Granite obelisk at churchyard entrance commemorates the parish martyr George Wishart of Pitarrow (see p.58).

Manse, 18th-century rear wing; dynamic entrance façade with spiky dormers and exclamatory chimneys added 1844, John and William Smith.

The old church square is enclosed by **Kirkton Farmhouse**, an 18th-century coaching inn, grey harled with wallhead chimney gablet. The box bed Robert Burns slept in is now a wardrobe. **Auchenblae School,** John Sim of Montrose, *c.*1889, single storey, E-plan. All three wings have crowstepped gables. Bold three-light fenestration on outer bays, topped by segmental pediments.

Manse, Fordoun.

AUCHENBLAE

Best appreciated from Gilbert's Hill. The generous main streets are flanked by a variety of 19th-century houses which remain distinctive yet harmonious in their colour and scale. There is little intrusive modern development on the main vista which has primary mansions on the lower part of the hill and single-storey-with-dormer cottages at the top, on Inverurie Street. It was laid out in its T-plan by the Earl of Kintore *c.*1770, designed as a flax-spinning mill town. The abandoned site of the mill is by the stream to the west of the village.

Left Auchenblae from Gilbert's Hill.
Below Denmill.

Denmill, Burnett Street, 19th century
With kiln and distillery-type vent at east end and an iron overshot wheel at the west end. **Village hall**, Monboddo Street, red brick with white dressings, displays a prominent circular barometer. The interior delights with its bespoke joinery, particularly the complex roof. Over the stream, former **Clydesdale Bank**, 1840s, distinguished porch decorated with heraldic panel; policies are complete, with walled garden, gatepiers and iron gates. **Thistle Inn,** early 19th

Top *The Hollies*. Above *Glencairn*. Right *Fordoun House*.

century, gable to street, with three windows and plain painted architrave to the central door. **Gowan Lee**, dated 1876 on gable, two upper windows cantilevered on stone brackets projecting into street.

The barely accented Market Square is dominated by the compact perfection of **The Hollies**, 1790, with three windows and four-panelled door facing neat garden surrounded by iron railings and gate. **Glencairn**, High Street, later 19th century, ashlar with contrasting dressings and imposing windows. Old red rubble shed in **Mackenzie Place**, *c.*18th century, has a notable flagged stone forestair and motley windows including some very small 12-pane sashes.

Cedar House, Kintore Street, early 19th century, fine consoled and pedimented doorpiece, distinctive dressed quoins.

51 **Fordoun House**, 1712

Dated on a window lintel, an austere but imposing three-storey, five-window gabled block, white harled, with incongruous modern glass porch. *A better sort of farmhouse; with a moderate outlay it might be made into a pleasant residence* (*New Statistical Account*, 1844). Formerly a dower house for Arbuthnott House, perched on a bluff, with remains of medieval homestead moat in adjacent trees. Cliff-like façade and narrow windows make it the Kincardine equivalent to Gallery, Angus.

Redhall House.

Redhall House, *c.*1825

For Revd Alexander Carnegie, elegant and low lying. Porch, flanking bays and three-window bow added to original two-storey harled house, *c.*1830.

Whinhouse, 1899

Somewhat incongruous latecomer to this strongly vernacular parish, its Tudor half-timbered gables redolent of Surrey Arts & Crafts. Apparently built for the Fettercairn distillery manager.

RCAHMS

The judge James Burnett, Lord Monboddo, 1714–99, wrote *The Origin and Progress of Man and Language,* a study of evolution anticipating Darwinian theory: he suggested that men were originally monkeys whose tails had worn off by constant sitting. He was sought out by Dr Johnson and Boswell on their tour of the Highlands in 1773: *the magnetism of his conversation easily drew us out of our way.* Boswell noted *Monboddo is a wretched place, wild and naked with a poor old house, though … there are two turrets which mark an old baron's residence* (*Tour of the Hebrides*). Robert Burns also visited Monboddo and was very taken by the Lord's youngest daughter 'Fair Eliza': *There has not been anything like her in all the combinations of beauty, grace and goodness the great Creator has formed since Milton's Eve on the first day of her existence* (letter to W Chalmers, 1786).

Left *Monboddo House, 1973.*
Below *Monboddo House, 2000.*

Geddes

52 Monboddo House, from 1635

A delightfully perky, two-storey harled manor house, with turrets on two corners, punished by time and the efforts to revive it. The main house has date stone on the west gable with the arms of Irvine and Douglas, 1635. In the west basement the enormous fireplace of the old kitchen implies an earlier tower.

James Matthews added massive Scots Baronial wing, 1886–7. 'Enabling development' by Alistair McAlpine and Christopher Davey, 1977–8, renovated the core of the old house (with the loss of the original panelling to hall), removed the baronial extension, converted the outbuildings into three houses, and constructed seven mini-Monboddo harled and turreted 'executive' homes in the immediate policies. Although quite generously spaced, these impudent castlettes, like a circle of mushrooms, rob Monboddo of its dignity.

Geddes

Monboddo housing.

53 Phesdo House, 1814–15, John Smith

A crisp and clean surprise in this parish of uniformly warm brown sandstone, built of gleaming silvery granite ashlar, imported from Aberdeen. Serene Greek Revival, U-plan with main block to south and wings to north west and north east. Two-storey main block has tetrastyle fluted Doric portico, pilastered angles and

John Smith, 1781–1852, unfairly dubbed 'Tudor Johnny', was the prolific Aberdeen Town Architect from 1807. Son of the builder William Smith, he was the first Aberdeen architect to be trained in London. Effective classical monuments are the North Parish Church, now Aberdeen Arts Centre, and the screen on Union Street across St Nicholas Churchyard. In medieval style, he completed the west wing of King's College quadrangle, Trinity Hall on Union Street, St Clements at Footdee, Aberdeen, Old Balmoral (1834–9) and Banchory House, along with numerous other churches.

Phesdo House.

The old manor house of Phesdo was held by the Falconers of Haulkerton. The present house was bought by the Aberdeen advocate, Alexander Crombie, renovator of Thornton. It was then bought by the Gladstones of Fasque who used it as a hunting lodge for the latter part of the 19th century; it was commandeered for German POWs in the 1940s, became a youth hostel and has now reverted to private ownership, after substantial renovations in the 1970s.

Corbel, Pitarrow Farmhouse.

The Wishart family produced many distinguished members: four bishops (St Andrews, 1273–9, Glasgow, 1271–1316, 1337, and Edinburgh, 1662–71), and George Wishart, one of the seven Protestant martyrs, burnt hideously at the stake in St Andrews before his gloating enemy Cardinal Beaton, in 1546. The Cardinal was stabbed to death shortly afterwards by Wishart's supporters.

consoled ground-floor windows. Within the portico, recessed consoled doorpiece has oval lower panels and friezes of interlocking circles on the central panels. West and east elevations, three bays with platformed roof. On the west wing, timbered veranda supported by slim coupled columns and lattice-work spandrels.

Screen of Corinthian columns in entrance hall, repeated in the drawing room. Principal rooms have elegant Greek Revival chimneypieces. Stables and lodge also John Smith, *c*.1815 (demolished). Restored 1970–1, Bird and Tyler.

Pitarrow House (demolished 1802) Three clues remain to its existence: the doocot, substantial garden walls with bee boles and the carved stones reset into the walls of **Pitarrow Farmhouse** and barns. On the house, stone inscribed *IW: ID 1599* commemorates the Wishart and Douglas families; two bold head corbels on barn gables, of the same type as at Balbegno (see p.48). Hidden under the wainscoting of the old hall were bright paintings of a papal procession in Rome, showing cardinals, horses and St Peter's Church.

54 **Drumtochty Castle**, 1813, James Gillespie Graham Elongated U-plan, for George Harley Drummond, with long south front and two wings projecting backwards into hillside. Flaky grey stonework of north-west wing shows this is the earliest section, onto which Graham added the south and east sections in warm brown ashlar. South front rears up over the steep valley, with central semicircular tower. The south-west, four-lobed tower is based on Caesar's Tower, Warwick. West elevation has projecting central turret. Modern stairtower in angle of main block and north-west wing. Perched on a terrace, the house stretches along the side of its steep and narrow glen. Its stunning

use of the site and bold asymmetry make Drumtochty one of the most romantic mansions in this area.

Left *Drumtochty Castle.* Above *Interior, Drumtochty Castle.*

The main public rooms are ranged at ground level along the south side, backed by a spine hall, top-lit through a perpendicular-traceried lantern. The entrance, an arch between shallow octagonal angle turrets, is on the east wing, which is mainly occupied by the double-height dining room. Most windows have original wooden tracery sashes and the interiors are intact.

A small, gothic, *very plain house in the cottage fashion, covered with thatch,* already stood here when James Gillespie Graham was hired to add a perpendicular finish to the exterior and design the great hall and lantern. John Smith of Aberdeen was paid for a large building programme here in 1815–16 but the exact division of labour between the two architects is not clear. House restoration, 1974–5, Jenkins and Marr; major landscape renovation including new lake, 1999–2001, by owner Charles Anderson.

Drumtochty Castle Stables, 1850, Thomas Mackenzie
Neo-Tudor H-plan with square central tower, now stylishly converted to flats. Original diamond-pane glazing replaced by vast expanses of plate glass, effectively used over the great doorways.

St Palladius Episcopal Church, 1885, Arthur Clyne
For Revd J S Gammell, then owner of the castle, its mighty semicircular apse and ornate pencil tower by south transept create a satisfyingly compact and varied massing of volumes. Top of tower has dwarf gallery with effusively carved foliage capitals, large sculpture of St Palladius on exterior of south transept. Inside, lofty wooden wagon roof, aisleless, plastered nave and rubble-faced apse delicately lit by close-spaced lancets (colour p.68).

A *snug and unpretending cottage* formerly stood on the site of Drumtochty Castle. With its picturesque view of trees, steep-sided glen and burn, surrounded by lofty mountains, *it may be questioned if the view of the present lordly mansion ever gave half the pleasure to one possessed of sound judgement and taste which the former humble cottage afforded* (New Statistical Account, 1845). In 1822 the castle was bought as an occasional hunting lodge by the Gammell family of Countesswells. In the First World War it became a hospital. Bought by the Norwegian Government, it was used as a centre for escaping Norwegian refugees, 1939–45. It served as a celebrated prep school from 1948–68, attended by the authors Allan Massie and Elspeth Barker, where her novel *O Caledonia* was largely set. It became a restaurant, before reverting to a private house in 1981.

Drumtochty Castle Stables.

Set on a low haugh, St Palladius Episcopal Church is a fittingly romantic complement to the castle above, and an imaginative rebuff to the parish church at Fordoun (see p.54).

Glenfarquhar Lodge.

Glenfarquhar Lodge, *c.*1900
Built for Sir Sidney Gammell on the site of
Glenfarquhar Castle, home of the Falconers, Earls
of Kintore. Now part of the Rudolph Steiner
settlement of Templeton. Half timbered and boldly
painted with red gloss detailing. Adjacent modern
wood cottages also brightly painted in red and
yellow, in accordance with Steiner's colour theory
for developing a harmonious mental attitude.

Arbuthnott House.

In a sheltered, fertile glen, the house seems almost cut off from time. Its tree-lined valley is the creation of 33 lairds of Arbuthnott, caring for the policies in unbroken succession for almost eight centuries. Approaching and entering this little realm is like walking down a time tunnel, with each step leading progressively backwards from the classical gateway, through the urbane Georgian house front, into the baroque living rooms and gardens, out at the back to the medieval remains, while at the church a microcosm of medieval piety survives intact.

Development of Arbuthnott House, 1242–1756.

ARBUTHNOTT
55 **Arbuthnott House**, from 1242
Evolved over eight centuries, its dramatic
location on a triangular bluff between two small
rivers accounts for its trapezoid courtyard plan.
External triple chamfered plinth from *c.*1242 on
north wall of small building on the north side of
the yard (also found on east wall of the church).
Hall House from 1420, with kitchen and store
below, hall and chamber above, forming the
central section of the south range. Sir Robert, 12th
laird, 1475–90, completed the Hall House,
*decorated ye head yairoff with evis galreis and
batilment as ye forme is of Castellis,* extended it to
the west with a block called **The Twin**, and built
a kitchen block on the north side of the yard.

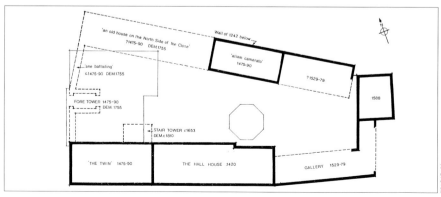

Kitchen cellars were lit by crosslet gunports, possibly related to those at Ravenscraig (see *Banff & Buchan* in this series), also late 15th century.

Inside, Robert Arbuthnott, 3rd Viscount, created two outstanding **drawing rooms** in the The Twin, *c*.1682–5, probably to please his wife Lady Anne Gordon, daughter of the Earl of Sutherland. Their rich plaster ceilings, covered with wanton foliage and surrounded by deep mouldings, can be paralleled at Brodie, Kellie and Fyvie, of which Fyvie by Robert White, 1683, is the closest (see *Gordon* in this series). Fragments of a painted ceiling, *c*.1650.

Fashionable classical west front created for John, the 5th Viscount, by John Ferrior, 1755–7. Gable end of The Twin (on the right) dictated conservative handling of this scheme. To create a symmetrical front, three-storey, three-bay centrepiece, bound by rusticated groins and a pediment, is flanked by north gable wing matching the old south block. Various demolitions and additions finally linked the 1750s' north wing and central block to the south wing, while the central top-lit staircase provided access to most of the house in 1795–1800.

The garden terraces were laid out in the 1680s. **Garden house**, a classical stone aedicule with pointed roof and moulded doorpiece extending to gatepiers with fluted bases and ball finials. Ostentatious classical **bridge**, 1829–39, stone balustrade and urns on the buttresses. **East Gate** is flanked by aristocratic Greek Revival temples, one of which is a lodge. Entrance is completed by a curved ashlar screen and Greek-style iron gates. **Arbuthnott Mains Farm**, dated 1792 on the gables, a typical three-bay, two-storey farm, but with attitude. Giant order pilasters terminate the main building, flanked by six arcaded bays of stabling.

56 **Arbuthnott Parish Kirk**, from 1242
One of the most exquisite and unusual relics of the medieval church in Scotland, combining an unmolested location, high-quality building and evidence of secular piety linked to religious devotion. Dedication to St Ternan suggests an early Christian origin, together with the site, above a steep slope leading down to the stream. Sloping chamfered plinth on the outside of the church also found on the 13th-century part of Arbuthnott House. Early English arches separate the chancel and aisle from the nave. Western octagonal turret and two-storey Lady Chapel or **Arbuthnott Aisle** added by Robert Arbuthnott,

Sir Robert Arbuthnott, 12th laird, commissioned James Sibbald (d.1507) to make three books, a Psalter, Missal and Book of Hours between 1471 and 1491, all surviving in Paisley Museum (colour p.69). Robert also *buildit ane Ill* [aisle] … *verie gorgiuss both in craft and materiallis, for it is a biggin off fyn hewin stone cassin further in squarit butreis going up to the head and having little turrattis upon yame* … [He] *forsaw that this costlie building in no wayis suld be hurtful to his puir tenantis sua he carrit the stonis, lyme and all the rest of the materiallis with his avin horses and wald tak no help off his tennantis as the custom was.* Description by Principal Alexander Arbuthnott of Aberdeen University, *c*.1567, whose genealogical account provides early terminology for Scottish building.

From top *Plaster ceiling, west drawing room; Bridge; East Gate; Arbuthnott Mains Farm.*

Top *Corbel, Arbuthnott Aisle.* Above *Medieval effigy.* Right *Arbuthnott Aisle.*

On the *c.*1900 glass in Arbuthnott Church:
It had fine glass windows, awful old, with three bit creatures of queans, not very decent-like in a kirk, as window-pictures. One of the queans was Faith, and faith she looked a daft-like keek for she was lifting up her hands and eyes like a heifer choked on a turnip.
Lewis Grassic Gibbon, *Sunset Song*

Lewis Grassic Gibbon's grave.

*c.*1500, a magnificent example of private devotion and patronage on the eve of the Reformation. Supported by four prominent buttresses with pinnacles, elaborate **corbels** (one with Arma Christi) and tabernacles for statues of saints. Refined ashlar throughout.

Entered through an arch in the south wall of the chancel, polygonal south end has three widely splayed lancet windows. Recumbent **effigy** of a medieval knight in armour (perhaps Hugh le Blond, the 3rd laird who began the church) lies in the stone vaulted chapel, upon a 16th-century tomb. Narrow spiral stair leads to the priest's room above with three square windows furnished with window seats, the largest barred with a massive iron grille. Small stoop and trefoil-headed aumbry. Nave burnt 1890; sympathetic restoration, 1896, A Marshall Mackenzie, few original features survive (colour p.70).

Buried in the **graveyard**, James Leslie Mitchell, famous under his pen name of Lewis Grassic Gibbon (1901–35), author of *A Scots Quair,* the trilogy beginning with *Sunset Song.* He lived in the hilltop croft of **Bloomfield**, Blaewearie, now somewhat tidied up but still isolated and wind-whipped. *Out of the world and into Blaewearie they said in Kinraddie, and faith! it was a coarse land and lonely up there on the brae* (*Sunset Song*).

57 **Allardice Castle**, mid-16th century
Perched on a terrace, surrounded on three sides by the deep meander of the river. The bold massing of simple turrets and chimneys gives Allardice a muscular sculptural quality. Stepped L-plan, once forming an enclosed courtyard with walls on the other two sides. Entry into the courtyard via a pend through the main block. Most effective and striking is the compressed series of label-corbels supporting the staircase which rises in the re-entrant and then staggers outwards to form a second stairturret and slender window turret flanking the cap-house. This intense curving composition is bolstered by the adjacent wallhead chimney from the great hall. Later wing with date stone 1695, offset to the west, adds to the attractive series of receding planes and terminates in a slender round turret.

Above *Allardice Castle*. Left *Kair House*.

Allardice Castle was first mentioned in 1297 when Walterus de Allardice signed the Ragman Roll, an oath of fealty to the English king, Edward I. Duncan Judici, who became Allardice of that Ilk, was granted the castle by Robert the Bruce, and his family stayed there until 1800 when the heiress married into the Barclays of Ury. The long line died out when Captain Barclay-Allardice died in 1854, and by then the building was *a ruin*. The castle is restored as a private home.

58 **Kair House**, later 18th century
Clean-faced classical mansion whose metropolitan grace comes as a surprise in this parish otherwise dominated by rugged medieval structures. The Georgian façade of Arbuthnott House and Mains Farm appear overworked by comparison. *A goodly looking plain house. It is remarkable as being among the first works of the late celebrated Adam, the architect* (attribution by G Robertson, early 1800). Two-storey ashlar central block with pediment over all three bays, built for George Kinloch of Kair. Centre of the house is top lit. Symmetrical single-storey wings linked to the house by recessed bays which provide a discrete movement to the façade. House neatly echoed by **stables** which have a projecting central bay with pediment and side wings of two bays.

Kair Stables.

By marriage in 1492, Glenbervie House passed from the Melville family to Sir William Douglas. It was sold to Robert Burnett of Leys in 1675, whose family sold it to Sir William Nicholson of Mergie in 1721. It remains in the private ownership of his descendants.

Below *Glenbervie House.* Middle *Glasshouse in walled garden.* Bottom *Sundial.*

Single-storey, early 19th-century lodge has projecting bow-fronted ends linked by a recessed bay. Here too, the clean geometric forms of cones, rectangles and semicircles make a balanced composition.

GLENBERVIE
Its main strategic importance was that a route to the Dee, the Cryne's Cross Pass, led through this parish.

59 Glenbervie House, from 14th century
Two generous round towers with conical roofs flank the three-storey, four-bay main block. The old house, white harled and totally unadorned apart from a decorative parapet, is quietly dignified, although the Victorian extensions to the rear and side are more demonstrative. Edward I stayed at the manor here in 1296 and the round towers may originally derive from 14th-century courtyard castle but the plan is unusual. If the house is 1680, it contains its predecessor within. Ground floor solidly vaulted into four chambers with corridor along the back; towers have cross loops with bottom roundels. Central scale-and-platt staircase leads to the Victorianised upper apartments, where the old solar retains its 17th-century wood panelling. South and west wings, 1854. South tower given a dramatic parapet and pepperpot helmet, 1854, restored to its original shape, 1965.

The walled garden has notable early wooden **greenhouses**, from 1850, summerhouse with bottle-glass floor and *boiserie* bench, and **sundial** with fluted baluster shaft supporting a table dial dated 1767. Doocot, 1736, with ball finial on pyramid roof.

Geddes

National Gallery of Scotland/ D Wilkie

Geddes

Jonathan Smith

Top *Stonehaven from south*. Middle *Market Square, Stonehaven*. Above *Forebank House, St Cyrus*. Left *The Burying of the Scottish Regalia by D Wilkie*.

Jim Henderson

Geddes

Charles McKean

Top *Dunnottar Castle.* Right
*Reconstruction drawing of Dunnottar
Castle.* Above *Fettercairn Distillery.*
Below *Inglismaldie, Marykirk.*

Geddes

Top *Public Hall and fountain, Fettercairn.*
Above *Carron Tea Rooms, Stonehaven.*
Left *Kincardine Castle Road.* Below
Catterline in Winter by Joan Eardley.

67

Right *Gannochy Bridge*. Below *St Palladius Episcopal Church, Drumtochty*. Middle *Parish Church and St Palladius' Chapel, Fordoun*. Bottom *Stonehaven Open-Air Swimming Pool*.

1.5m

Top *Gourdon harbour.* Middle *Old Parish Church, Dalmaik.* Left *Book of Hours, Arbuthnott.* Above *Cottage, Arbuthnott.*

69

Geddes

Jonathan Smith

Above *'Faith' stained glass window,
Arbuthnott Parish Kirk.* **Right** *Deserted
croft on the Fettercairn/Banchory Cairn o'
Mount road.* **Below** *Lauriston Castle.*

William Newlands

Top *Fasque*. Left *Dalmaik Old Manse*.
Above *Drum*. Below *Library, Drum*.

Top *Low tide, East Coast, by James Morrison.* Above *Lodge, Dess House, Kincardine O'Neil.* Left *Sundial, Park House.* Below *Bridge of Feugh and Tollhouse.*

Only the chancel remains of Glenbervie **Old Parish Kirk**, converted into the **Douglas Burial Aisle**, 1771. Altar tomb from 1591 is topped by a mural monument of 1680 recounting the genealogy of the Douglas family back to 730. In the churchyard lie the ancestors of Robert Burns: William Burness of Bogjorgan and James Burness of Brawliemuir, but their stones are badly weathered.

Old Manse, late 18th century, central gable chimney to front, later additions at rear. **Parish Church**, *soncy and broad*, 1826, perpendicular gothic, with pinnacles at the angles and on the belfry. By the kirkton, **Glenbervie Centre**, 1998, Brian Cheyne for Macphie and Co. food manufacturers. Low rise, with a wide oversailing roof and large expanses of dark glass windows, landscaped into the outstanding scenery, a looming but not dominating modern presence.

The character of **Drumlithie**, the old hand-loom weavers' village, is now mainly appreciated through its tiny, winding street plan. Most of the old cottages have been modernised with roof extensions, pebble dash and big windows. The miniature circular **steeple** of 1777, with belfry and cap renewed in 1880, was used to regulate the weavers' working hours.

Angleside, the old parsonage, linked to **Westhame**, and the long, low **Melrose Cottage** retain some of their 18th-century appearance. **Episcopalian Chapel** was razed to the ground by Butcher Cumberland in 1746; the modest harled replacement, 19th century, built by Charles Brand of Fordoun. **Free Church**, 1850, now converted to two-storey house.

DEESIDE
Leaving the rich agricultural landscape of the Mearns, the guide now proceeds westwards up the Dee valley.

Left *Parish Church*. Top *Douglas Burial Aisle*. Middle *Old Manse*. Above *Glenbervie Centre*.

Its steeple made Skite [Drumlithie] *the laugh of the Howe, for feint the kirk was near it. Folk said for a joke that every time it came on to rain the Drumlithie folk ran out and took in their steeple, that proud they were of the thing.*
Lewis Grassic Gibbon, *Sunset Song*

Drumlithie steeple.

60

73

Opposite right from top *Boswell's Monument; Mansefield; Old Schoolhouse; St Devenick's-on-the-Hill.* Left *Banchory-Devenick Parish Church.*

Portlethen: *Notwithstanding every endeavour on the part of the minister to get rid of the nuisance of public-houses, we still have eight in the parish, none of which can be said to be necessary* [except at] *Portlethen, for which, being situated on a rocky coast where wrecks sometimes occur, there is a plausible pretext.*
New Statistical Account, 1845

BANCHORY-DEVENICK

This parish stretches from the scenic leafy south bank of the Dee, successfully protected from Aberdeen's urban encroachment, to the rocky, boggy coastal plain by Portlethen, designated to accommodate thousands of new homes for the city. South Deeside, for its entire length, has no villages but is punctuated by a series of stately mansions set in fine parkland overlooking the river.

PORTLETHEN

A small fishing village until Aberdeen oil arrived. **Parish Church**, *c.*1840, spacious, airy box, harled and slate, on a prominent site asserting its old-fashioned decorum over this sprawling new settlement.

Portlethen Academy.

Portlethen Academy, Bruntland Road, 1987, Walter Scott for Grampian Regional Council One of the most successful buildings in a developmental wasteland. Its broad, clean lines are formed by white pebble-dash walls, large areas of window broken up by small square panes and red sheet roofing. An axial, top-lit corridor, filled with seats and plants, forms the central spine of the school, a sociable shelter in a windswept district.

Below *Glebe Court*. Bottom *Cameron Controls, Badentoy Industrial Park.*

Glebe Court, 1988, Squire Associates Repeats these clean geometric lines and square windows and is suitably landscaped to provide welcoming sheltered housing.

    Badentoy Industrial Park, 1990s, Stevenson Associates, laid out like a garden city, with formal lime avenue approach, some good postmodern units. **Varco International**, 2000, Jenkins and Marr, its full-height atrium created by the clever capture of space between the offices and warehouse.
    Cameron Controls, postmodern temple façade with columns and pediment. Landscaped setting

for **Cairnwell Ring Cairn**, *c.*2000 BC, reconstructed 1995. Contrast this with the raw tackiness of Kincardineshire's earliest retail park, **Asda**, 1985.

Boswell's Monument, 1862
Landmark circular stone tower, three storeys high, dedicated to John Boswell of Kingcausie who *lived to transform the natural barrenness of the estate into luxuriant fertility.* Originally capped by an open crown vault, like King's College Chapel (see *Aberdeen* in this series).

61 **Banchory-Devenick Parish Church**, 1822, John Lyon
Simple gothic box, with four bays of lancet windows, birdcage belfry, harl and slate; altered 1865 and 1929. In churchyard, both a 19th-century cast-iron **mortsafe** and mort house. On a typical early Christian site on rising ground above the Dee, dedicated to St Devenick, an early missionary.

*As **many poor** people could not afford to pay the expense of watching, Mr George Barclay designed two massive iron chests or safes for placing around the coffin when lowered into the grave. The iron safe was lowered by block-and-tackle and the grave filled up. Six weeks later, when it was considered that decomposition had made such progress as to preclude the chance of a visit from the body-snatchers, the grave was opened and the safe removed.*
J A Henderson, History of the Parish of Banchory-Devenick, 1890

Mansefield, mid-19th century
The old manse, now smartly suburban, double pile harled villa with exposed quoins, window margins and stringcourses. Ashlar porch with round arch and solid parapet links each wing. Low pitched roof with oversailing eaves.

Old Schoolhouse
Main block early 18th century with bulging boulder plinth and later additional wing; schoolhouse attached to rear, early 19th century, original woodwork inside. A permanent structure befitting a school whose records go back to 1711.

St Devenick's-on-the-Hill, 1844, Cousin and Gale
Plain, oblong Free Church, with round-topped windows and bell turret. The original dormer windows allowed for a pleasing conversion into two two-storey family apartments, *c.*1991.

Above *Pictish stones in garden wall,
Beannachar.* Right *Beannachar.*

62 **Beannachar**, 1840, John Smith
Sprawling organic plan with many gables and
mullion windows, the former Banchory House,
for Alexander Thomson, serves as an important
reminder of Smith's similar but demolished
work at Balmoral, 1834–9. Elizabethan style,
two storey; date stone, 1621, and possibly
foundations incorporated from previous house.
Rescued in an almost ruinous state in 1978
(after a serious fire removed most of the
interior), it is now a Camphill-Rudolph Steiner
community school.

In the garden wall, Class 1 **Pictish stones**
recovered from Dunnicaer (see Dunnottar p.25).
Significantly, they are not stele but plaques or
panels, perhaps used in some construction, like
the bull panels from Burghead, Morayshire (see
The District of Moray in this series).

Rose, 1994, Camphill Architects, a Steiner-style
house in the gardens, has curved rooflines and
canted chimney.

Above *Rose.* Right *Ardoe House.*

Ardoe House, 1878, James Matthews
Scottish Baronial at its most exuberant, for
Alexander Ogston, soap magnate of Aberdeen,
with dense massing of features around the
entrance, gleaming silver granite and slate.
Bartizaned *porte-cochère* attached to square four-
storey tower with projecting bay windows and

corbelled round turret. Lavish interior, classical panelled foyer, massive wooden carved staircase with pre-Raphaelite style window glass; mosaic floor, Jacobean plaster ceilings. Flimsy glass ballroom extension, 1980s, Thomas Craig; new grey granite bedroom wing, 1991, blends in more harmoniously. Hotel since 1947. Appropriately emphatic **East Gatelodge**, 1878, with crowstepped gables at either end and over the front porch.

East Gatelodge.

Left and below *Riverbank.*

Riverbank, 1990s, Ron Gauld
Timber-clad chalet for the architect himself reveals total floor to ceiling glass wall on river façade. Open-plan sitting, eating and sleeping on bare wood floor. Informal gravel flower garden with Beth Chatto inspiration, which only permits plants naturalised to a raised beach. An uncompromisingly modern minimalist house which shows how a bold gesture can succeed in this ultra-conservative riparian location, fusing a traditional fishing lodge with Zen simplicity.

MARYCULTER
Bounded to the north by the leafy riverbank of the Dee, and spreading southwards through open farmland. The Knights Templar established a preceptory at Maryculter between 1221 and 1236. In 1535, the Knights' chapel of St Mary became the **Old Parish Church** until demolition, 1787. The low outline of the walls survives and a few carved stones including a stoop.

63 **Maryculter House**, medieval and later
Set on a bend of the river amid stately beech trees, the historic white harled core is almost lost among recent commercial accretions, but the romance of the Templars and the river make this a popular venue for weddings.
The vaulted basement of the Templars' lodging forms part of the 18th-century Ha' House (1735 on skewputt), two storey, harl and

After their dissolution in 1312, the Templars' lands were taken over by the Knights of St John of Jerusalem. At the Reformation, the lands of Tilbouries, Maryculter, Kingcausie, Blairs and Auchlunies were feued off; the remainder of the Knights' lands were acquired somewhat later by the Menzies family.

Maryculter House.

slate, with projecting gable-topped central bay, now open to the rafters. Additional wings from 19th century and 1980s make a courtyard facing the river. Adjacent 'enabling development' from 1991, in the park once described as *embosomed in wood; the beauty of the situation is great*, has produced a crop of mini castle-wise 'executive' homes with baronial shields over the doors, round turrets, dormers and gables (see also Monboddo p.57).

Scout Headquarters, late 17th century
Two storey, harl and slate, five bays. Distinguishing early features of small, deep-set, narrow windows and coved chimney copings. The 18th-century **Old Corn Mill** by the Mill Inn originally belonged to the Templars, and survives as a shop and farm buildings, with the over-shot 64 wheel being restored. At the kirkton, **Parish Church**, 1787, enlarged in 1882 with organ transept to south and church hall to north, contains original dense and intimate box pews and balcony.

Camp Cottage, late 18th century
The old schoolhouse, with single-storey classroom attached. Some original woodwork inside.

Top *Old Manse*. Middle *Old Corn Mill*. Above *Parish Church*. Right *Kingcausie, c.1800*.

The church bell, made by Mears and Stainbank of London in 1896, arrived inscribed with the words Sancta Maria, Ora Pro Nobis *much to the disapproval of the Kirk Session who had the offending words removed by a workman.* Third Statistical Account, *1988*

Below *North front, Kingcausie*.
Bottom *Kitchen yard, Kingcausie*.

65 **Kingcausie**, from 16th century
Oblong seven-bay house whose baronial additions on steroids completely transformed its quietly noble charm. Original core rebuilt after fire, *c.*1680: front door with deep bolection mouldings on south side, where the two-storey central block was flanked by two wings – the massive yew hedges of *c.*1680 indicate where they ended. New north face, extra floor and steep hipped roof added, 1750, dining room retains panelling from this period. North front door moved into the garden wall by David Bryce when he added the frontispiece, dormer pediments and massive corner towers (resembling Montreuil-Bellay in France) in 1851. The curved wall, lean-to and domestic scale of the **kitchen yard** are particularly attractive.

Philip's Cottage, mid-19th century
For the Kingcausie estate overseer, picturesque,
like a dolls' house, central door, two diamond
lattice windows, oversailing slate roof, moulded
chimney tops and neat garden wall.

Eastland, mid-19th century
Granite, three bays, two storeys, canted dormers,
oversailing slate roof. Interesting classical details
on the octagonal columns and reeded architrave
of the wooden porch, and dignified pilasters in
hall. Formerly a priest's house with chapel in
upper bedroom.

Auchlunies, from 17th century
Attractive house, converted twice at
unsympathetic times. E-plan, with 18th-century
wings, two storey, harl and slate. Some original
panelled doors but interior is mostly 19th
century. Converted into three apartments, 1960s,
with typical plywood doors.

Altries Free Church, 1844, William Henderson
Romantic ruin in a copse, with bellcote, three
pairs of round-topped windows and dressed
granite margins.

   Altries, a complicated house concealing a 16th-
/17th-century core with 1m-thick walls at centre.
The house was turned to face the river, c.1840,
when the bow-fronted west wing was added.
Interior mainly mid- and late 19th century.

From top *Philip's Cottage; Eastland;
Auchlunies; Altries.* Left *Blairs College
from south.*

66 Blairs College
Formerly the principal Roman Catholic seminary
in Scotland, it is more like an entire village than
an institution. The closely packed silver granite
buildings create an inward-looking world,
imparting strength and discipline. Older
buildings are tucked into the back of the complex
so that one's first impression is of the New
Chapel and institutional New College.

Blairs College: above north entrance; right Menzies House (right) and Old Chapel (left).

Blairs, originally the seat of John Menzies of Pitfodels, an ardent Catholic, was given to the church as a seminary in 1829. Catholic training had carried on more or less in secret since the Reformation at Scalan and Aquorthies (see *The District of Moray* and *Gordon* in this series) and the Blairs estate allowed for the expansion which occurred after Catholic emancipation in 1829. The college closed in 1986 and the future use of the site is still uncertain, but the chapel continues to function and the outstanding collection of Catholic art is preserved here, in a museum open to the public. This includes medieval vestments and the memorial portrait of Mary, Queen of Scots.

New Chapel.

Menzies House, 18th century
Three-storey-and-attic mansion, five remaining bays on plain northern elevation. South elevation, facing into yard, has four-storey projecting gabled wing. Interior not original. Extended to south, 1827, John Gall. Abutting north block, 1854, five-stage circular stairtower and conical slate roof.

Old Chapel, early 19th century
A pleasant classical interlude in this mainly gothic world. Three bays with pediment, blind round-topped windows with square windows above. Red brick on east face, the rest, dressed granite. Inside, four fluted and reeded Ionic columns with gilt volutes, beneath saucer dome with oculus above. Remodelled 1827, John Gall.

New College, 1898–1902, Alexander Ellis and R G Wilson
U-plan range with entrance to north: entrance tower forms a massive porch, five storeys high topped by four corner bartizans, linked by open arched belfry with crown, inspired by King's College Chapel (see *Aberdeen* in this series). Three-storey main façade, granite ashlar on a rusticated plinth. Inside the decoration is sparse, especially in the residential areas, but the hall is panelled and the library with gallery has a ribbed timber ceiling. Addition to north west of the old complex, 1906.

New Chapel, 1899, Robert Curran
Funded by Mgr Lennon of Liverpool, hall church in grey Rubislaw granite with pink tracery; buttressed tower and slender steeple on the north-east corner. Tall and graceful traceried east window. Interior surprises with rich textures and colours, covered by hundreds of panels of different coloured marble, 1910–11, C J Menart. Chill polished stone offset by barrel-vaulted timber ceiling and the exuberant woodwork

around the chancel, seats, spiky gothic baldacchino over the altar and framing statues of saints. Good stained glass by Mayer of Munich.

DURRIS
The parish stretches from its sheltered kirkton on the banks of the Dee through vast acres of forestry plantation to the twin hills of Cairn-mon-Earn and Mongour whose communications masts provide a landmark for all lower Deeside.

St Comgall's Parish Church, 1822
An ancient dedication and site with semicircular graveyard beside the river. Rectangular box with round-headed windows and bellcote. Interior, refurbished 1897, has murals of a phoenix and pelican at the east end and delicate cast-iron balustrade leading to gallery. **Fraser Burial Aisle**, rebuilt in 1869 by the Mactier family from part of the old church, inscribed 1587 on a skewputt, has a cast-iron mortsafe and 1594 Fraser wall tomb.

Above *Fraser Burial Aisle.* Left *The Glebe.*

The Glebe, 1844
Former manse, a stately and generous U-plan house with Doric portico and well articulated walls, its deep pavilion roof reminiscent of Archibald Simpson. Similar corbels above the windows are found at **Kincluny Farmhouse**.

The cottages of the kirkton, especially **Nos 2, 3 & 7** make a picturesque group beside the burn. Their canted chimney tops suggest they are 18th century. **Old Bridge of Durris**, 18th century, springs organically over the gorge of Sheeoch. **Kirkton Mill**, 18th century, has deteriorated rapidly since it last worked in the 1960s. The waterworks are interesting as the stream drove two wheels, for a two-storey meal mill with drying kiln and adjacent sawmill.

Kirkton Mill.

Durris House.

The early house at Durris belonged to the Fraser family. The raid of the Marquis of Montrose in 1645 set fire to *the place, lauche bigging and haill cornes, and spolzeet the haill ground of horse, nolt, scheip and other goodis.* Cosmo Innes the distinguished antiquarian was born here in 1798; in 1871 it was bought by James Young, discoverer of paraffin.

Below *Durris House Stables.*
Bottom *Keith's Tower.*

67 **Durris House**, from 16th century
Imposing complex of buildings latched onto a fine L-plan tower house, three storeys and garret, consisting of main block and stair wing topped by cap-house set in luxurious grounds filled with rhododendrons and specimen trees. Re-entrant filled by later wing. Vaulted basements show plan of original building which seems to extend below much of the later wings as far as the square eastern block. Great hall, on the first floor of the tower, unusually has two fireplaces. Probably built after the raid by the Marquis of Montrose in 1645 when he burned the previous house.

In 1824 Archibald Simpson added a north-east wing for the Duke of Gordon, extended in 1835 and 1838 for Anthony Mactier, a merchant from Madras: an almost Palladian three-storey, three-bay cube, with projecting central bay and Venetian window breaking into the pediment; low pitched hip roof. Large bald *porte-cochère* with plain round arches on each side. All removed, the present east end has an unhappy amalgam of rooflines and spindly porch on iron brackets. Used as control centre for Aberdeen area civil defence, 1960s; converted into apartments, 1980s.

Durris House Stables, 1830s
Masculine and confident, H-plan, rubble and slate, pilastered and pedimented centre bay surmounted by doocot tower. Conversion into apartments, 1990s, by Michael Gilmore, has saved the structure and given the building a strong postmodern appearance, with Georgian fanlights downstairs and diamond-pane windows upstairs. **Durris Gardener's Cottage**, 19th century, U-plan with overhanging eaves and sandstone lintels.

Keith's Tower, 1825, on an eminence above the river, ashlar gothic with battlements, built by the 4th Duke of Gordon to commemorate his acquisition of the Durris estate after an acrimonious lawsuit.

The traditional tower house has two fanciful new interpretations in Durris, each built for a different purpose and with different results.

Strathieburn, 1986, Ron Gauld
Lapped by a brook, the L-plan tower for the architect himself thrusts above the lip of its dell location to command an outstanding view of upper Deeside. Part harled, part ashlar, it has a different character on each face owing to various recycled cut stones. The 17th-century style entrance front uses stone from the burnt-out wing of Crathes Castle and Craiglarach in Aboyne, while the 18th-century style west front, with sash windows and gable comes from Culter papermills. Disposition of façades is particularly appropriate since the big windows face the view. Interior similarly ingenious, re-using beams from the paper mill and old panelling in the dining room; living room is on the first floor to enjoy the view.

Balfour Tower, 1991, Michael Rasmussen
Here the challenge was to produce a tower house for Ian Watson, for the same cost as an up-market executive home, with all modern conveniences. Result is honest and effective: three-storey L-plan house, pink harled, with two corner turrets, vaulted ground floor, cosy and panelled first floor. Materials are modern, but agreeable patina will form.

DRUMOAK
Evolved from the holy well and church of St Maik by the river ford at Dalmaik, gradually shifting its community up to Drum and then towards the centre of the parish at the present village.

68 **Old Parish Church**, Dalmaik, 18th century
Roofless ruin with older masonry – in 1790 it was *so old that nobody knows when it was built: it has had frequent repairs* (*Statistical Account*). Functioned on two levels, with corbels at the west end supporting a gallery and external stairs on both the north and west sides. Bell, 1790 (colour p.69).

Top *West façade, Strathieburn.* Middle *Entrance, Strathieburn.* Above *Balfour Tower.*

Opposite left *Drumoak Parish Church.*
Right from top *Drum Chapel; walled
garden; East Lodge; Schoolhouse,
Drumoak.*

Drum was politically sited to guard the
Cryne's Cross Mounth, the pass leading
from Laurencekirk over the Mills of
Drum ford to the north. The secluded
religious settlement at **Dalmaik**, lost in
trees by the river and passed by as
progress overtook the parish, still
sustains the holy atmosphere and
strategic importance of the ancient river
crossing.

*Drum: right south wing; below by
Timothy Pont, 1590; bottom tower.*

Robert the Bruce gave the royal hunting
forest of Drum to William de Irwyn in
1323 and the castle was already built.
Alexander Irvine built the Drum Aisle in
St Nicholas Church, Aberdeen: his tomb
of 1457 was later moved from there to
Drum Chapel. The 9th laird, Alexander,
Sheriff of Aberdeen, who built the
Jacobean wing, lent money to King James
VI and donated a bursary to Marischal
College. The castle suffered in the Civil
War, being invaded four times by
Covenanters, Lady Irvine being evicted
with only *two grey plaids and a couple of
work nags.* The estate never recovered
from these losses, and it was seriously
curtailed by financial troubles in 18th
century. From then many lairds became
lawyers or served in the army.

Dalmaik Old Manse, *c.*1761
Renovations, 1988, and harling conceal a
venerable house; windows have round-
chamfered openings, chimneys are coped and
skews are straight. West and south wings also
18th century (colour p.71). Adjacent farmyard has
18th-century bothy, rubble with cherrycocking
and coped chimney. Steading has slit windows
and bulging boulder foundations.

69 **Drum**, from 1280
The mighty tower stands like a doorstop,
commanding westward access up the river – a
case study for the development of the Scottish
tower. Massive rubble walls (at least 2m thick)
have rounded corners, and crenellated
battlements project slightly on corbels. Windows
are tiny, except for one large insertion; access was
by an external wooden stair or ladder to first floor.
Stone barrel vaults to cellar below Laigh Hall
(now library) and High Hall; stair between cellar
and High Hall within the wall thickness, upper
storeys reached by ladders. One of the earliest
Scottish towers, like Hallforest (see *Gordon* in this
series), but unlike the rest was continually in use
and occupied by the Irvine family until 1975.
　　Jacobean U-plan south wing, 1619, two storeys
above basement, with carved dormerheads. A
stately five-bay symmetrical block, flanked by
square angle towers and one turret staircase in re-
entrant angle, it shows the evolution from
vertical to horizontal living. Reminiscent of
Fettercairn House (see p.50). Entrance doorway
inserted and main windows enlarged *c.*1800.
Enclosed court on north side, like Muchalls (see
p.22), with 16th-century brewhouse. Gateway
and entrance block with main staircase added to
north side, 1875, David Bryce (colour p.71).
　　Inside, Jacobean hall with gallery above now
divided into smaller rooms, most of the detailing

*c.*1882, John Bryce, except 17th-century stone fireplace in the Business Room. Library (former 13th-century hall) was converted in 1840, plaster vaulted ceiling covered in heraldic shields. A stupendous homoerotic self-portrait of Hugh Irvine (1783–1829) as Angel Gabriel, distracts all eyes from the notable book collection (colour p.71). *National Trust for Scotland; open to the public*

Drum Chapel, 16th century
Simple box with crowstepped gables and re-used medieval head corbels, restored 1856. Glass by Hardman of Birmingham; great silver statue of the Virgin brought from Augsburg, 1897. **Walled garden**, 1796, laid out as a display of historic roses in 1991, with the gazebo based on one at Tyninghame. **East Lodge**, dated 1892, sturdy mini-baronial with vigorous round turret on corbels and finely carved heraldic panel; addition, 1954, by Walker and Duncan.

Drumoak Parish Church, 1835–6,
Archibald Simpson
Harled with ashlar margins, this box church makes economical use of its prominent location. Perpendicular gothic features thinly applied with spindly angle buttresses and tracery window at south end. Simple perpendicular pine interior with Doric columns under balcony.

Schoolhouse, *c.*1900
Generously proportioned with overhanging eaves, groups of triplet windows and substantial Arts & Crafts interior.

Drumoak House, 1836, John Smith
This old manse is the up-market model for several other houses up the Dee: Coull Manse, Corrachree and Wester Coull. Three bays wide, sash windows, dormers and gable windows in the

According to the minister in 1845, Drumoak church was *finished in so neat, and comfortable, and even elegant manner, that it is the best specimen in this part of the country of what a parochial church ought to be* (New Statistical Account). It has just to be said that, as compared with most of the *barn-like structures of Aberdeenshire, it is something, but as nothing compared with our rural churches in rural England, and what our churches in rural Scotland might well be made.*
G M Fraser, *The Old Deeside Road*, 1921

attic, and most elegantly, the sweeping staircase projecting from the back in a round tower. Fine original interior woodwork and plaster. Originally had stone porch with Doric columns. Fine detailing marred by 1960s' pebble-dash.

Old Manse Steading, 2000, converted by John and Marion Donald, a model of how to treat these frequently overlooked buildings, skilfully retaining original openings and materials.

Top *Drumoak House*. Above *Park House*.

The manse is a handsome and commodious building, pleasantly situated by the side of the river … it cost L.800. In front is a terrace garden … To that little spot the present incumbent has carried upwards of 2,000 cart-loads of earth collected from the banks of the river… and the heritors, who always study his comfort and convenience, have enclosed it, in the most liberal manner, with a stone and lime wall which cost L.105. New Statistical Account, 1845

Below *Old West Lodge*. Bottom *New West Lodge*.

70 **Park House**, 1822, Archibald Simpson
A long, low white house of Arcadian grace for William Moir of Aberdeen. It succeeds, by its muted understatement, in being monumental and small at the same time. Austere neoclassical façade, two storeys with projecting end bays and seven blind central bays upstairs. Tetrastyle fluted Greek Doric portico with wreathed frieze, white-painted stucco (colour p.72).

Interior, with floor-length sash windows, exploits outstanding location by the river. Domed entrance hall with Ionic scagliola screen. Rooms delight with their variety: dining room has coved ceiling and wood-grained doors; saloon has delicate Adam-style fireplace and double doors leading to the oval withdrawing room. Spine corridor allows all state rooms downstairs to face the river, backed by services to rear. Modest top-lit staircase leads to two major bedrooms in end bays and lesser bedrooms along blind corridor.

Old West Lodge, c.1822, Archibald Simpson
Modest harled cottage graced by proto-Doric wooden porch, with entablature and columns bound by rustic lattice, as a reminder of the big house. **New West Lodge**, late 19th century, fussy over-designed gothic, with exaggerated gables and formal ashlar. **Park garden**, c.1823, has semicircular crinkle-crankle wall of granite lined with warm brick, fine classical gates and gatepiers. Decayed subterranean **mausoleum**,

1868, with octagonal umbrella vault, surmounted by pink granite obelisk and entered through doors with elaborate wrought-iron hinges. It commemorates James Kinloch of Jermyn Street and Bombay. Charming early 19th-century **fishing lodge** has hipped pantile roof, harled walls and chimney. An idyllic retreat.

Left *Fishing lodge*. Below *Park Bridge*. Middle *Drumoak Free Church*. Bottom *Sunny Brae*.

Park Bridge, 1854, John Willet, engineer, James Abernethy, ironfounder
Two graceful cast-iron arches with arcaded spandrels. Built by the railway company to supply passengers for Park Station, with tollhouse on the north side.

Drumoak Free Church, 1880, Ellis and Wilson
Tightly massed, strong granite church; bold grouping of lancets incorporated in transepts, entrance gable and bellcote produces a rhythmic if schematic gothic façade. Now a community hall.

Sunny Brae, Cowie Partnership, 2000
Designed for Deryck Forbes, building contractor: traditional Edwardian-style mansion, built from solid recycled Aberdeenshire granite, with Portuguese granite facings. Sits low on the hillside thanks to monumental earthmoving efforts.

Mills of Drum, from 18th century
The **Corn Mill** existed in 1644 when Montrose encamped here, the present L-shaped collection of buildings converted sympathetically by the owner to a house, 1996. Single storey, granite rubble and slate, with wheel and lade still in situ. **Meal Mill**, brick-lined granite kiln dated 1830, adjacent to miller's house, was originally two bays plus door, extended to three bays with dormers.

The ancient parish of Banchory-Ternan, crossing both sides of the Dee and Feugh, takes its name from the 5th-century Saint Ternan who founded a small ecclesiastical centre at the old kirkton (now in Banchory town), typically by the river and with a holy well.

Right *Crathes Castle by R W Billings, 1852.* **Above** *Music room, Crathes Castle.*

Tower houses built by the Bel family are *Scotland's finest and most distinctive contribution to western architecture.* H Gordon Slade, *Proceedings of the Society of Antiquaries of Scotland 108,* 1976–7

Crathes is an early example of the spectacular clutch of local castles embellished by the Bel family of Midmar. The father, George, died in 1575, and his two sons John and David were also architects. Among their other houses are Midmar, Fraser and Craigievar (see *Gordon* in this series) characterised by an imaginative and sensitive handling of the dramatic rooflines and subtly modulating upper elevations.

Crathes Castle.

BANCHORY-TERNAN

71 Crathes Castle, from 1553

Six-storey L-plan, with vaulted basement and hall, harmonious gentle pink harling. Above great hall (vault boss 1554, Venetian windows inserted 1870s) the elevation begins to mutate and almost explode at roof level, added by the Bel family, complete in 1596. Stringcourse wanders like a loose thread under turrets and windows; half-round stairturret changes into square clock tower which corbels out to a crenellated viewing gallery; square cap-houses juggle with asymmetrical crowstepped gables; cannon-barrel gargoyles project everywhere; each façade glancing off light and shadow in unpredictable ways. Viewing gallery on west front acts as screen concealing need for twin roof across the great span of the main block (colour p.121).

Inside, ingenious arrangement of rooms, hall and laird's room above, both double height, rising adjacent to suites of smaller rooms on mezzanine floors. Above, the long gallery, with contemporary

panelled heraldic ceiling, stretches full width of top floor. Most significant features are the vigorous and bright 16th-century painted ceilings (colour p.121): ornamental fragments in hall; nine Muses and seven Virtues in one room and Nine Nobles in another. Outstanding collection of Scottish oak furniture mostly bought for the house in early 17th century. South wing added early 18th century, enlarged 1894, R G Wilson; burnt 1966, rebuilt by Schomberg Scott.

The **garden** is *deeply retired in luxurious woods* (Billings, 1852). Its yew hedges, planted at beginning of 18th century by Sir Thomas Burnett, deserve to be considered as architecture, their dark noble outlines contrasting with the airy pale pink harling of the house. **Doocot**, early 19th century, rebuilt 1937, square rubble with pyramid roof, inset with carved panel from the Houses of Parliament. Polygonal **gazebo**, a good example of local *boiserie*, rustic pine trunks and shingle roof (colour pp.121, 122). Near the house, **horse-mill**, with its distinctive conical roof, rare in Deeside where most mills were water powered; converted to restaurant. **East Gatehouse**, 1858, somewhat overdesigned crowstepped gable, above round-topped triplet window shaded by cornice on consoles. *National Trust for Scotland; open to the public*

The sequence of bridges at **Milton of Crathes** over the Coy Burn sum up the history of Deeside transport in one compact view: narrow rubble and cobble humpback packhorse bridge, 18th century, the only surviving bridge of the Old Deeside Road; turnpike bridge, 1802; the railway bridge, 1852, square, granite, dressed copes; main North Deeside Road bridge on concrete pylons, 1939; flat concrete slab farm bridge, late 20th century (colour p.122).

The **Milton** itself is a large collection of rubble and dressed stone buildings arranged around a courtyard, surrounded by working lades, sensibly converted in 1990s into a retail outlet.

House of Crathes, 1972, Michael Thomson and Schomberg Scott
Z-plan, two storey, harl and slate with 12-pane sash

Sir Thomas has by care and skill subdued the genius of the place for by planting firs and other trees with the hand he has covered forbidding crags, laid out gardens and clothed it with amenity.
Macfarlane's Collections

Topiary, Crathes Castle.

Below *Milton of Crathes.* Left *House of Crathes.*

The **Burnett** family were given their estate by Robert the Bruce in 1323 and have lived here ever since. With the land and status of Royal Forester, the king gave Alexander Burnett the ivory Horn of Leys, carved and decorated with semi-precious stones, still kept in the castle. A successful marriage to Janet Hamilton in 1543, and fall-out from the Reformation added considerable estates from Arbroath Abbey, enabling Alexander Burnett to begin building the castle. It was wholly remodelled by his grandson, also Alexander. Astute politics saved the property from damage in the Civil War, keeping intact the riches of interior decoration just recently installed. The Queen Anne wing was added when Sir Thomas and his wife Margaret Douglas produced 21 children in 22 years. Major General Sir James and his wife Sybil Smith, influenced by William Robinson and Gertrude Jekyll, developed the remarkable colour-coded garden in the 1920s.

89

Top *Mill of Hirn.* Above *Entrance, Raemoir House Hotel.* Right *Raemoir House Hotel.*

Smith's interiors at Raemoir, including the oval dining room, are formally classical; Kelly's are more rustic pitch pine panelling, reflecting the house's later use as a shooting lodge for the Cowdrays who also bequeathed fine 16th- and 17th-century furniture.

Below *Ha' Hoose.* Bottom *Cluny-Crichton.*

windows and low stairturret in the re-entrant. Moulded sandstone margins to front door. Understated but ample house with pleasing complexity provided by the stepped roofline. Built for the Burnett family after the fire of 1966 encouraged them to move out of the castle.

Mill of Hirn, 19th century
Rubble and slate, picturesque group with crowstepped gables on kiln and miller's house fronted by wooden open-work lattice. Recently renovated and converted to private house.

72 **Raemoir House Hotel**, from 18th century
Imposing mansion set in fine parkland, central tall and plain block has a similar elevation to Birkhall, 1715 (see p.132). West wing with classical pedimented entrance porch and gable by John Smith 1817 and 1844. Gabled east wing and considerable interior woodwork, 1927, William Kelly for the Cowdrays of Dunecht. Lands surrounded by miles of the formidably compact and accurate drystane dyking for which the Dunecht estate is famous.

Ha' Hoose, Raemoir, 1715 or earlier
Two storeys, T-plan with projecting wings and two oval lights above door. The normal long narrow hall house is balanced by the possibly later front wings with hipped roofs lower than the main ridge. Interior gutted and modernised, 1923. An unusual early example of a minor laird's house, originally belonging to the Hogg family.

73 **Cluny-Crichton**, 1666
Small three-storey L-plan country seat with square tower at re-entrant. Date and name panel the only surviving detail, all other walls and openings sadly robbed. Built on older site by George Crichton of Cluny just after his marriage to the daughter of Robert Douglas of Tilquhillie, rather old-fashioned by this date and perhaps never completed. Deserves a new lease of life.

Woodend House, from late 17th century
Beautifully sited fishing lodge on serene stretch
of the Dee, apparently a gracious Regency villa
but concealing much more. The chaotic roof
indicates its many stages of enlargement. Rear
kitchen block has thick walls and bulging rock
plinth and (once separate) male servants' block
with open forestair. At the front, bow forms a
shallow porch with strong Greek key mouldings,
also found at Park House (see p.86); Doric
columns form screen to lounge. Originally part of
the Crathes estate.

Cairnton House, 1920s
Substantial white-painted fishing lodge, the river
front amply supplied with windows set beneath
twin sweeping gables.

Top *Woodend House.* Above *Cairnton House.* Left *Inchmarlo.*

74 **Inchmarlo**, from 1750
Imposing, if somewhat bald and heavy, classical
mansion for John Douglas of Tilquhillie.
Originally a two-storey, five-bay house with
extensive wings to rear and massive high-pitched
hip roof; reconstructed, 1823, John Smith; third
storey raised and flat roof with balustrade added,
1850; earlier burnt east wing replaced, 1987; rear
reconstructed and house restored by Skene
Enterprises as a nursing home.

Original entrance hall with Doric columns led
into main formal rooms on each side. Present
three-part windows in centre bay replace a
classical portico. In this district it presents an
unusually formal and imposing classical façade
but the mainly modernised interior disappoints.

South Lodge.

South Lodge, early 19th century
Attractive hip roof with over-sailing eaves.
Extension on right, 1923, G R M Kennedy and
Partners. A good example of extending a tiny
lodge into a useful house without losing its
character. Deeply concealed in Inchmarlo park is
an extensive **retirement village**, 1990s. The

Queen Victoria Park.

secluded location and totally new community gave an opportunity to provide imaginative new styles of accommodation. Instead a banal spread of bungalows prevails. Within this complex, **Queen Victoria Park**, 1990s, Russel Parker, provides sheltered housing around courtyards with Orientally inspired gardens. Two-storey blocks with pantile roofs, deep balconies and bold fenestration. Exterior detail and landscaping is trim and stylish.

BANCHORY

Spreads across the south-facing bank of the Dee at a point where the coastal climate changes to the brisk and brighter weather of the uplands. Its historic heart lies in the area of the old churchyard where the 5th-century St Ternan probably converted a pagan well for Christian purposes. The Old Deeside road passed along at this level, beside the manse and down to the Coble-heugh Inn at the ferry crossing (see p.96). The town took its modern appearance after an effective bridge was built over the Dee in 1798 and the new turnpike (present main road) was constructed above the old hamlet in 1802. Feus along the new road began to be developed between 1805 and 1809, the town becoming a burgh in 1885. In 1853 a railway station (demolished 1971) was built on the old kirkton and the town flourished as a resort for day trippers from Aberdeen.

It is a pleasant, straggling looking place, with many tasteful villas, favourite resorts of Aberdonians.
Groome's Ordnance Gazetteer, 1882

Unquestionably nature has done a great deal for Banchory; the marvel is that the [19th] century had begun before the nucleus of a town had been founded in such a delightful situation. But its builders have failed to make use of its natural advantages, and cannot be congratulated on their success in laying it out.
A I McConnochie, Deeside, 1900

Watch house, Banchory Kirkyard.

75 **St Ternan's Parish Church** (demolished 1775) Old stones incorporated in **Douglas Mausoleum**, inscribed *J D 1795 M A* for John Douglas, 23rd laird of Tilquhillie and wife Mary Arbuthnott. Smoothly worn early Christian grave marker cross built into west wall. Adjacent two-storey **watch house**, 1829, like a fat circular tea caddy, with conical roof, chimney and bellcote for the old bell, 1664, by Peter of Ostend. Restored and reharled, 1998, Alistair Urquhart, mason.

Celtic Cross Nursery, 1798
Former manse, two storey, harl and slate, dominated by classical porch *c*.1900, and several intermediate additions to rear. Spiked finial dormers are like those on **68 & 70 Station Road** (former school and schoolhouse), *c*.1840. Celtic cross found during road works nearby inserted into garden wall.

76 **East Parish Kirk**, 1824, John Smith
Typical Smith perpendicular, similar to Nigg and

Udny (see *Aberdeen* and *Gordon* in this series), built to provide more space and to align with the new turnpike. Distinctive Smith features include diagonally set buttresses, four-storey tower with firmly proportioned door, simple tracery windows and spindly pinnacles. Most of Smith's galleried interior is gone. Chancel, 1928–30, George Bennett Mitchell, an inspired addition with finely moulded chancel arch, generous windows and outstanding oak furnishings, organ, font and chancel seating crisply carved with medieval tracery and vine scrolls. St Ternan's bronze bell, excavated by the railway in 1863 and now in the church, possibly an early Christian relic or fake.

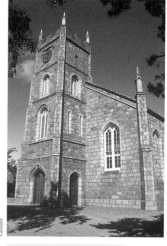

Arbeadie Hall, 19th century
Particularly imaginative conversion into flats, 1994, by James Hammond, of a plain ecclesiastical building into a distinctive landmark. Discrete roof extensions at the rear provide additional space while the new windows with ladder tracery, part mirrors and part glass, draw the sky down into the façades.

Top *East Parish Kirk*. Above *Arbeadie Hall*. Right *High Street, 1890s, by G W Wilson*.

High Street
Unsightly concrete road lamps and intrusive road and shop signs have been replaced by new versions with a more sympathetic scale and colour, 1999, Aberdeenshire Council. As a result the street has almost recovered its aspect of the 1890s.

Bellfield Retirement Home.

77 **Bellfield Retirement Home**, High Street/ Dee Street, *c.*1900
Bold polygonal tower and spire provides a fitting sense of place to main town junction. Remainder of the sub-baronial south façade has crowstepped gable, bay windows and inharmonious modern rendered east wing.

67-68 High Street.

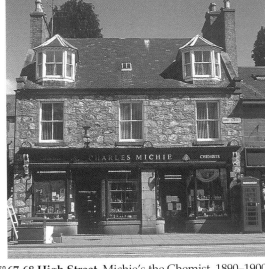

George Davidson of Inchmarlo Cottage, 1859–1939, invented a plane in 1897, six years before the Wright brothers. Based on the concept that the machine would rise vertically by flapping its wings like a bird, the plane crashed after a few minutes' trial in Burnett Park. He went on to invent a 'gyropter' in America in 1911. It looked like a double-disc flying saucer. He predicted ominously that one day his type of helicopter would be used for *dropping loads of dynamite on enemy country.*

Below *Scott Skinner Square.* Bottom *Burnett Arms Hotel and West Church.*

Crime in Banchory is negligible; the citizens are law-abiding and there is very little drunkenness. Still, football coupons find their way into many good homes, while the predatory proclivities of boys prove troublesome, especially in the season of mellow fruitfulness.
Third Statistical Account, 1949–55

78 **67-68 High Street**, Michie's the Chemist, 1890–1900 While the three-bay upper storey with four-pane sashes and canted dormers above are a common formula from this period, the detail surviving on the shopfront is exemplary. Windows are supported by cast-iron columns with tiny Ionic capitals; glazing curves at the entrances; timber frieze has dentilled cornice and elaborate consoles. These motifs have been recreated recently elsewhere down the street. Gilded mortar and pestle hang from a decorative bracket.

79 **Scott Skinner Square**, 1993, James Hammond A modern solution to the old problem of the 'straggling looking place'. Named after the Banchory 'Strathspey King', Scott Skinner (b.1843), composer and remarkable fiddler, the square provides an enclosed community space away from the traffic, with shops, housing, a library and museum. Buildings are pebble-dashed granite composite with dominating angular concrete tile roofs; hard landscaping. A sombre echelon of wooden porches rise up to the bell tower. Outlines impress on the large scale, but this potentially intimate enclosure is short on smaller-scale detailing which would relate it more closely to the High Street.

Burnett Arms Hotel, *c.*1830
Generously dignified hotel with fine classical aspirations which, together with the adjacent church, defines the character of this end of town. Pediment over three central bays, scagliola Ionic

portico. East wing added *c*.1851, interior radically modernised *c*.1980.

Douglas Arms Hotel, *c*.1800
A bit worse for wear, coursed rubble (formerly harled) with fine classical moulded pediment over entrance. These two hotels represent the commercial aspirations of the two local lairds.

80 **West Church**, 1879–85, James Souttar
Cheery pink-and-white tower of this former Free Church is a hallmark of the High Street. Gothic, first pointed, with 30m high baronial bell tower and broach spire.

St Ternan's Episcopal Church, 1851, William Ramage
Small oblong nave and chancel with belfry. Unassuming exterior, nicely detailed interior, with cross-braced roof on Early English corbels; well-moulded chancel arch and sedilia. Victorian stained glass.

St Columba's RC Church, 1931
Low oblong with polygonal turret at west end, small Romanesque windows with ashlar facings.

War Memorial, The Square, 1923, William Kelly
Miniature obelisk shrine of simple smooth granite, influenced by Lutyens. Excellent proportions and lettering. Stands in front of the Tudor-gothic **Burgh Buildings**, 1838, former Lady Burnett School.

81 **Castle Airy**, Watson Street, early 19th century
Narrow but stately on a precipitous site now curtailed by shops below, substantial Georgian mansion of coursed field stones and ashlar margins; two full storeys with dormers set into roofline on bow-fronted sills.

82 **Elizabeth Cottage**, Woodside Road,
late 19th century (colour p.124)
Joyous escapee from the frontier architecture of Braemar, former reputedly Roman Catholic T-plan chapel, re-erected incongruously in bourgeois Banchory. Prefabricated corrugated iron with decorative pierced timber bargeboards, timber finials and lacy cast-iron veranda with swept eaves.

Top *Douglas Arms Hotel*. Middle *War Memorial*. Above *Castle Airy*.

Balnacraig, Corsee Road, 1887
Respectable stockbroker solidity, pink granite, square crenellated entrance with three-storey baronial tower, like **Druimdarroch** next door.

Above *Wynndun*. Right *Glen o' Dee Hospital*.

Dr Otto Walther developed the 'Nordrach Treatment' for tuberculosis in 1888 in the German Black Forest. This required plenty of fresh air, sunshine and rest for the patients and Walther's sanatorium was designed to fulfil these needs. Dr David Lawson of Banchory decided to copy the treatment and the building here at Nordrach on Dee. The granite came from the Hill of Fare but the bulk of the building, its timber frame and cladding, came directly from Germany. *All bedrooms face south, and are heated by steam pipes, lighted by electricity, and fitted with hot and cold water supply; the floors being covered with material which readily ensures absolute cleanliness.* Somerset Maugham based his story 'Sanatorium' on his stay here. It was converted into the Glen o' Dee Hotel in 1938 but resumed as a tuberculosis clinic in 1948. With the construction of new geriatric wards behind the main block, the sanatorium stands empty, its timber reaching the end of its useful life and ready for demolition. Any future developments here should take advantage of the secluded location to develop dynamic and expressive woodland architecture in memory of the Black Forest precedent.

Below *Tor-na-Coille Hotel*. Bottom *Banchory Lodge Hotel*.

83 **Wynndun**, Corsee Road, mid-19th century Whimsical fantasy house, with compact domestic proportions. Bow front, conical belvedere with wooden balcony, deep eaves and wooden porch, harling with granite margins.

84 **Glen o' Dee Hospital**, Corsee Road, 1900, George Coutts
Designed to clear the lungs and lift the spirits of tuberculosis patients, when the only cure was rest and fresh air. Cheerful balconies, windows and sunshine provide the medicine in a luscious park full of ozone from the pine trees. Three storey, timber with central granite tower standing between nine gabled bays. Variety provided by open timbering on some gables, canted slate roofs on others, and long stretches of open balconies (colour p.125). Rooms all face the sun while the rear accommodates corridors, services and stairs. Totally functional in its day, would health authorities have the courage to construct such an uplifting and radical building now? Large expanses of clay-tile roof and low walls of Scolty and Morven wards for the elderly, 1987 and 1990, Aberdeenshire Health Authority, are no doubt practical but establish little relationship with the rich wooded landscape.

Tor-na-Coille Hotel, Inchmarlo Road, 1873
Two-storey-and-attic granite mansion built for Mr Thompson, a brewer. Plain façades lifted by cast-iron veranda with fluted columns and decorative balcony railings. Originally lacy cast-iron crest to roof ridge. Several interiors retain deep moulded Victorian plasterwork, ornate wooden fireplace in lounge.

85 **Bridge of Dee and Bridge of Feugh**
Banchory Lodge Hotel, early 19th century
On the site of 18th-century Coble-heugh Inn, by the river crossing and Old Deeside Road, the

property was redeveloped as Banchory Lodge by General William Burnett when the new turnpike was built up the hill, and the mighty beechwood gardens were laid out. Five-bay entrance block, with many later additions. West front with canted portico and web fanlight. Some original woodwork, especially in front hall, including lions' heads on door architraves.

Riverview House, 1994, Ron Gauld
Postmodern classical mansion for Mrs Margaret Jaffray, proprietor of Banchory Lodge, to complement the hotel in a highly sensitive location. E-plan, two-storey, harl and slate, with pediment and portico over entrance and granite margins on corners, a successful interpretation of a fine Deeside fishing lodge.

86 **Blackhall Gateway and Lodge**
Screen perhaps inspired by John Smith's façade to St Nicholas Kirkyard (see *Aberdeen* in this series). Originally the slender castellated arch was flanked by sets of Doric columns on each side, ending in square gothic 'sentry boxes' with crenellated parapet and lancet window. Gateway was surmounted by lifesize statue of a goat, the crest of the Russell family. Present contracted entrance includes polygonal gatehouse and conical turret, in turn inspiring **Deeview Apartments**, 1990s, Michael Rasmussen, with folksy pine-trunk porches and coarse artificial stone detailing.

Blackhall Castle, *c.*16th century
Originally a three-bay square tower with corbelled and crenellated parapet (similar in shape to Drum) and square corner turrets; two-storey house of irregular plan added 17th century. Porch combining classical columns and crenellations, echoed by gateway. Replaced, 1884, Charles Brand, for J T Hay, resolutely baronial, four-storey tower, corbels, crenellations, lower wing with crowstepped gables, crenellated porch; demolished 1946, its fine granite blocks used to repair bomb damage to the Houses of Parliament, London.

From top Riverview House; Blackhall Gateway and Lodge; Blackhall Castle before 1884; Blackhall Castle after 1884.

Dee Bridge, 1985
Energetic granite and reinforced concrete span with iron railings, replaces many predecessors, the earliest from 1799.

Rear elevation, Riverstone.

87 **Riverstone**, *c.*17th century
Began with a U-plan facing north to the River Dee. East wing has walls 1.3m thick, vaulted cellar, low-ceilinged ground floor, lofty *piano*

nobile with fine hall space, coved ceiling, now divided into two rooms. East and west wings end in thick-walled chimney gables with bulging plinths. Orientation reversed early 19th century to become bay-fronted villa facing south to the River Feugh. South front with canted bays created at same time as interior redesigned, with bold door architraves having the same lions'-head stops as Banchory Lodge (see p.96).

88 **Tollhouse**, Bridge of Feugh, 1790s
Pixie-wee and quaint, semi-octagonal bay front, very low second storey, house and rose gardens a notable complement to **Bridge of Feugh**, *c.*1790, Mr Russell of Blackhall, single segmental arch flanked by two storm-water arches, with cutwaters carried up to refuges. Built to withstand the frequent and impetuous spates over a rocky gorge, traversing a notable salmon leap (colour p.72).

89 **Firhillock**, South Deeside Road, late 19th century
Coarse sub-baronial, jollified by seaside cast-iron belvedere and porch. Square and round turrets, canted bays and bargeboards.

90 **Tilquhillie Castle**, 1576
The solemn echelon of its three cliff-like rounded corners and absence of any frills give Tilquhillie a stern masculine bearing. Modified Z-plan, three storeys and garret with semicircular stairturret in one re-entrant and slender corbelled stairturret in the other, built for John Douglas. All corners are

Top *Front elevation, Riverstone*. Middle *Bridge of Feugh*. Above *Firhillock*. Below *Tilquhillie Castle*.

rounded but distinctively corbel out to form a square base for the roof just below the eaves. Crowsteps and heraldic plaque frame provide the only external decoration to this rugged and practical design. Windows are small and irregular but most rooms are well lit. Vaulted cellar, spacious hall above. After the Douglases moved to Inchmarlo in the 18th century, the castle became a tenant farm, finally abandoned in 1948. The delicate and sensitive restoration by John Coyne has left an authentic patina to the building fabric, easily lost on more radical repair projects. Directly facing Crathes Castle over the river, it highlights the strengths of the tower-house concept, which succeeds in practical and aesthetic terms for both unadorned and deluxe versions.

Birkwood, mid-19th century
A picturesque fishing idyll. Single storey and attic, with elaborate bargeboards and ornate veranda, redolent of warmer imperial climes. Ornate Victorian interior (colour p.121).

Maryfield, early 18th century
Two-storey frontage, with vaulted laigh floor below. Intriguing because of its apparent height above the road, owing to the slope of the hill. On entrance side, a severe house, recently reharled, small windows.

91 **Knappach**, *c*.1840
Substantial and dignified gentleman's mansion, two-storey bow with flanking towers on east front. Harled with pink granite surrounds, now almost doubled in size with rear extension in same style, 1999.

Top *Rear elevation, Maryfield.* Middle *Knappach.* Above *Knappach Tollhouse.*

Knappach Tollhouse, *c*.1842
Single-storey bow with conical slate roof and incongruous modern extensions to rear.

Balbridie Farmhouse, late 18th century
Two storey, three window, plain, harled, with skews. Single-storey kitchen wing to rear. **Steading**, including whin mill, a particularly substantial example of rough stone building.

WATER OF DYE
At the top of Glen Dye the wide upland moors have recently been blanketed, amid much controversy, with conifer plantations. The summit, **Cairn o' Mount**, commanding a view over the Mearns, is named after the large pile of stones beside the road, a Bronze Age cairn. It

Balbridie Neolithic Timber Hall, *c*.4000 BC, perhaps the area's most important example of architecture, but invisible. Aerial photography in the dry summer of 1976 revealed striking crop marks of a large timber hall, *c*.24m x 12m, with bedding trenches and post holes which presupposed a massive roof about 10m high. Excavated by Ian Ralston, 1979. Other Neolithic houses in Britain, for instance in Orkney and Shetland (see *Orkney* and *Shetland* in this series), are much smaller and Balbridie is wider than other contemporary houses in northern Europe. It points to a sophisticated agricultural community, harvesting grain, using pottery and sheltering both the farmers and their animals under one roof.

was also the site of St Ringan's cross, a Pictish carving now in Marischal Museum, Aberdeen.

Spittalburn Bridge, late 18th century
Segmental arched humpback bridge, rough granite ashlar, picturesque on its lonely moor. Threatened by concrete Euro-bridge replacement. Brigands roamed here in the 18th century when the adjacent Spittal (ruin) provided essential shelter.

92 **Bridge of Dye**, 1680
The second-oldest bridge in Deeside after Bridge of Dee, graceful granite four-ribbed semicircular arch topped by parapet with triangular refuges. Forms a picturesque group with adjacent semidetached 19th-century cottages.

Glendye Lodge, from 1779
Built for the Carnegie family of Southesk as a shooting lodge, extended to rear, 1898, by the Gladstones of Fasque. River front, with central canted bay, is most coherent, lining up with Clachnaben behind and clinging to the cliff above the Dye.

Bridge of Bogendreip, 18th century
Segmental arch and rubble parapets, neatly straddling sandy, pine-clad bluffs.

WATER OF FEUGH
93 **Feugh Lodge**, 1812
Picturesque gothic agglomeration perched on the cliff edge. Harled circular central block with conical roof interrupted by crowstepped gable transepts, entrance through a smaller polygonal tower.

Top *Cottages, Bridge of Dye*. Middle *Bridge of Dye*. Above *Feugh Lodge*.

Scolty Hill Monument, 50ft rubble tower erected in 1842, to General William Burnett, builder of Banchory Lodge, a distinctive local landmark.

94 **Invery House**, from late 16th century
Low and rambling, set in a majestic park of beech trees by the river. Old north kitchen wing has bulging stone foundations and irregular windows. Classical east wing, *c*.1800, facing the idyllic river bank, provides a comely living room with two Venetian windows and pediment, matching modern south wing with dining room.

The beautiful parish of **Strachan** is presided over by the rocky knob of Clachnaben, its communications shaped by the Water of Dye and Water of Feugh. The route of this guide descends the Dye (B974) from Cairn o' Mount, then follows the Feugh (B976) up from Bridge of Feugh to Birse Castle and continues along the South Deeside Road, from Ballogie to Aboyne.

STRACHAN (pronounced *Straan*)
Overspill pressure from Banchory is well handled in the conversion of **Mains of Invery**, 1986, John Duncan, into several houses, each with

distinctive character and texture: harled tower
and bays, rough granite walls, varying low
rooflines. However, the integrity of Strachan, a
sunny but tight granite village, was shattered by
the addition of Dalbreck estate, 1990s, Matthew
Merchant, prominently sited with six substantial
houses of bright red brick and red tile roofs. Why
did the exquisite Feugh valley deserve an estate
more suited to Cheshire?

Invery House.

This handsome building was part of
the estate of the Douglas family of
Tilquhillie, except in 1812–65 when it
was owned by Henry Lumsden.
Latterly a hotel, now recolonised as a
private house.

Strachan Parish Church, 1867, James Matthews
Simple gothic box with lancet windows and
bellcote; derelict Free Church has large pointed
windows, transepts contained within the roofline
and gay traces of murals inside: pink and blue
walls with foliage borders.

Below *House of Strachan.*
Bottom *Tillyfruskie.*

House of Strachan, from 1631
Attractive former manse appears to be a three-
bay house between chimney gables, with
addition to west: in fact double pile with the
oldest section at the back, dated 1631 on
skewputt, the main front block, 1777, enlarged,
1828. The birthplace of Sir Thomas Reid, 1710–96,
author of *Enquiry into the Human Mind* and
founder of what came to be known as the
philosophy of common sense.

95 **Tillyfruskie**
Dated 1733 on skewputt, two compact wings and
courtyard wall provide shelter and simple
elegance. Small mansion built for David
Ochterlony, large proportion of wall to window;
windows chamfered; transomed fanlight; moulded

chimney caps. Single-storey south wing at right angles; courtyard completed by walls to south and east. Entrance gatepiers moulded with ball finials. Five-step mounting block and cheese press; some original woodwork but interior mainly 20th century. An unusually complete house for this period, may be compared with the slightly larger Shiels, Midmar (see *Gordon* in this series).

FINZEAN (pronounced *Fingen*)
The clear shallow waters of the Feugh once supported seven mills, a contrast to the untamed Dee which has none. Three surviving mills above Finzean present a rural idyll of man working in harmony with nature. Building materials are all local, scale is small and personal, the energy is free and sustainable and the hand-made equipment has the sensuous smooth patina of long use.

96 **Mill of Clinter**, from 1511
L-plan, two-storey, coursed granite meal mill with kiln and wheel; 1886 on window lintel, 1819 gable stone probably re-used. Complete but unused and decaying, good hand-wrought iron fittings.

Perciemuir Sawmill, *c.*1850
A collection of mainly wooden sheds and remarkably complex arrangement of several lades driving many wheels, for the sawmill, **turning mill** and generator. Restored 1980s, lade and retaining wall reconstructed, 1999. Started by Alexander Duncan from Huntly, still producing spurtles and broom handles of birch.

Bucket Mill, 1853
Start-and-awe wheel with double cast-iron frame. Lathes used to make buckets and hexagonal wooden floor blocks. Started by Peter Brown, whose initials and date 1855 are on his cottage on the opposite side of the road. Restored 1980s (colour p.123).

Top Mill of Clinter. Above Perciemuir Sawmill. Right Turning mill.

97 **Easter Clune**, 1719

Two-storey, three-bay house for Alexander Irvine (inscription over door: *AI MS 1719*), with small narrow windows on ground floor and 19th-century dormers breaking the roofline above; chamfered openings, moulded skewputts and thick walls. New three-storey wing at right angles, sensitively blending with the old, inscribed *GH JF 1988*, Peter Young, garret windows in gable. Stump of **Easter Clune Castle** in garden, said to have been a hunting lodge of the Archbishop James Stewart, Duke of Ross (d.1503).

Robert Dinnie, 1808–91, a master stonemason, wrote *An Account of the Parish of Birse* in 1865. Most unusually for any writer of that period, he includes a classic description of the construction of vernacular buildings in the 18th century, providing particular detail about the design of 'couples' (rafters) and the wooden lum (chimney).

Above Easter Clune. Left Mid Clune.

Mid Clune, 1995, Mike Rasmussen
Satisfyingly stony enlargement of a croft, new wing added at right angles to old, generous wooden dormers and spacious pine log porch. Notable new drystane dyke by Mike Kay.

Finzean House, 1954, Jock Lamb
First house, 1686, replaced by Victorian mansion with three half-timbered gables, 1860. Mainly destroyed by a fire, 1934. Current edition is undistinguished modern suburban design, with gable echoes of previous house. Imposing, two-storey **Home Farm Steading and stables**, late 18th century, with classical entrance archway, niches and pediment. **South Lodge**, 1858, with wonderful fantasy porch, barley-sugar timber columns and cushion capitals, supporting half-timbered upper storey. Triple F monogram on north west wall, to Francis Farquharson of Finzean (d.1876).

Finzean Church, 1863
Harled with four lancets and porch in south wall; comely simplicity echoed by the lancets in the vestry, 1934.

Joseph 'Frozen Mutton' Farquharson RA, the painter of views now popularised on Christmas cards, lived at Finzean House, 1918–35. His speciality was cold wet sheep in winter, atmospheric landscapes with a shiver factor (colour p.122). He used to sit all day in a small heated caravan, open at the back, so he could capture his bleak views accurately. Many of his paintings burned in the fire but several can be seen at Aberdeen Art Gallery.

Below South Lodge. Bottom Finzean Church.

Above *Birse Castle, 2000*. Right *Birse Castle by James Giles, mid-19th century.*

Birse Castle, built as a Gordon hunting lodge, fell into decline during the Civil War and by 1742, almost derelict, it became a den for caterans who ravaged the district. J R Heaven rescued it when only two walls remained. It stands defiantly now, on a stark podium, alone in a remote glen, surveying much the same view as the brigands shared, although it has now reverted to a hunting lodge, opulently updated for Sir Charles Pearson, 1999.

98 **Birse Castle**, *c*.1600
A bleak fastness in the wilderness, seat of the Gordons of Cluny, originally a square tower with round tower at one corner, changing to square cap-house on the angle. Upper angle turrets are supported by key corbelling like that at Knock (see p.133). Restored, 1905, for J R Heaven by George Bennett Mitchell who reroofed the building, fitted the interior and made the whole of the main turret circular. Extended 1930 for Lady Anne Cowdray by William Kelly who returned turret to its original square shape and created the convincingly gaunt three-storey east wing. **Kennels**, 1905, G B Mitchell, provide the dogs with their own witty turreted castle.

BALLOGIE TO ABOYNE BRIDGE
The route follows the B976 from Corsedarder to Aboyne, with a detour to Potarch. This covers Birse, a parish of sparse, scattered settlement, bounded on two sides by the rivers Dee and Feugh. From here the land rises through rolling hills up to the heights of Mount Battock. The passes through these hills from Angus, namely Cairn o' Mount and The Fungle, provided the main communication in the parish, stymied by the River Dee until 1813 when the bridge at Potarch was finally built.

War Memorial.

99 **War Memorial**, *c*.1920, William Kelly
Rock-faced granite with fine relief lettering, standing on the brow of Corsedarder Hill, near the ancient sentinels of plain monolithic **Corsedarder Stone**, and the heaped pile of **Corsedarder Cairn**, a Neolithic long barrow, 4000–2500 BC. **Glencatt House**, 1814, neat and bleak, three bays, harled and whitewashed, with coped chimneys.

Bogieshiel Lodge, 18th/early 19th century
An unexpectedly civilised house in such a wild
glen, used as the Catholic priest's house before
1850. Complex extensive plan, main portion
three-bay, two-storey, the south gable turns into
an elegant bow with pointed sash windows and
Gothick tracery.

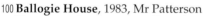

Top *Bogieshiel Lodge*. Left *Ballogie House,
1856*. Above *Ballogie House, 2000*.

*At that time (c.1800) several small
distilleries were at work in this Glen, and a
person having occasion to pass was
generally refreshed with a drop of the pure
mountain dew.*
Robert Dinnie, *An Account of the Parish
of Birse*, 1865

100 **Ballogie House**, 1983, Mr Patterson
Pleasant and compact neo-Georgian, for Colonel
John Nicol, rather St George's Hill, Surrey. Five
bay, two storey, low pitched roof and fanlight over
front door. Stamps a new generation on the
Ballogie Estate, bought by James Nicol in 1850.

The 18th century house was superceded by
James Matthews' 1856 mansion *presenting nothing
particularly interesting in an architectural point of
view* (Dinnie, 1865). An ungainly straggling house
with classical pretensions.

Below *Stables, Ballogie House*.
Bottom *Balfour House*.

Most of the prolific estate cottages were built,
and the remarkable exotic trees were planted in
the park during the 1850s–70s. **Stables**, 1832, for
Lewis Farquharson Innes, coursed granite, two
storeys, with a third storey in the tower over the
pend archway. **Allancreich Farm**, *c.*1850, lintels
on consoles over lower windows and
crowstepped gables. Farmyard behind provided
stabling for the horses on the drove road.

Muir Croft, Souter's Shop, *c.*1897
Vertically boarded shed for James Merchant with
large etched glass window, miraculously still
containing all the old shoemaker's equipment.
Owned by Birse Community Trust.

Balfour House, 1845
Overgrown cottage style, for Francis J Cochran,
an advocate in Aberdeen, *a very neat and handsome
dwelling*. Tudor chimneys, broad eaves;
symmetrical garden front has a rhythm of five
gables while the asymmetrical entrance front is
rather straggling.

Old Manse, from 1730
Began as a two-storey, three-bay house; *abundantly commodious* east wing added at right angles, 1790s; third wing added in the angle with block pediment gable, 1834. Substantial but additions lack coherence. Fine garden wall contains a Class I Pictish stone.

101 **Birse Parish Church**, from 1779
Rectangular box with richly moulded birdcage **bellcote**, *a most substantial and commodious edifice, superior to most*. Extensively altered and repaired, 1854, Matthews and Mackenzie; chancel added and interior redesigned, 1937, George Bennett Mitchell, enhanced by the colourful narrative glass of Douglas Strachan. Significant medieval tomb slab incised with two-handed sword, battleaxe and cross.

Top *Bellcote, Birse Parish Church.*
Above *Balnacraig House.*

The lintel at **Balnacraig House**
(*II–IHS–CG–1735*) provides many clues to its origin. James Innes and his wife Catherine Gordon were staunch Catholics and their Jesus initials on the door are a rare and defiant proclamation of their faith. After Culloden, in 1746, Captain MacHardy and the Redcoats came to arrest James (who was lurking in the hills behind) and burn the house. Catherine pluckily pointed out that the house belonged to their son Lewis who had no involvement with Bonnie Prince Charlie and thus the government would be responsible for any damage to the property. She then invited the restless troops in and plied them with a feast until they were *dreedfa' fu* and they eventually staggered forth with one intoxicated guard wearing an earthenware pot on his head. James witnessed the resolution of the crisis from the bushes.

102 **Balnacraig House**, 1735
One of the most architecturally and historically significant early houses in Deeside, now almost derelict. Long, narrow, two storeys, harl and slate, five bays with wallhead gable and chimney rising above central bay, bulging rock plinth, moulded skewputts and chimney caps. Forms a courtyard with two detached later 18th-century wings, completed by a garden framed with four stone gatepiers and ball finials. Finely carved front door has rich bolection moulding and classical lettering. Downstairs windows, with chamfered margins, each have sockets for three vertical bars. Interior has been remodelled. West wing, moulding to skewputts and chimney cap; east wing, haunched gables, replacement mansard roof and pair of lancet windows at one end, used as a Catholic family chapel. Formerly this contained a secret priest's hole and 'dool chamber', a death room designed to be near the chapel. **Cattle Court**, early 19th century; ball finials and birdcage bellcote, removed from chapel wing.

Potarch Hotel, 19th century
Comfy matching hip-roofed extension with
sympathetic window frames added to
rectangular wing, 1992, Gerry Robb. **Old
Smiddy**, Potarch, 19th century, long and low,
ending in a ball-finial gable above a mill race. An
effective conversion for domestic use, retaining
the industrial outline of the old building.

103 **Potarch Bridge**, 1811–13, Thomas Telford
Three graceful squared granite arches, refuges
over the cutwaters (colour p.125).

KINCARDINE O'NEIL
The first settlement here was begun by St Erchan
whose holy well is now enclosed in an ashlar box,
1858, with curved top, finial and lion's head
water spout. In 1228 the lands of Onele were
assigned to Thomas Durward who built a bridge
to facilitate the north/south route across the river
from Cairn o' Mount; his son Alan founded the
hospice for travellers attached to the east end of
the church, 1233.

Old Parish Church, c.14th century
Finely moulded 14th-century doorway in the
north wall suggests construction after the
church was made a prebend of Aberdeen
Cathedral in 1338. Exposed foundations reveal
the oblong box was formerly twice its present
length, incorporating two-storey hospice at its
east end, which appears to have been
demolished in 1625 with lancets from the old
east gable inserted into the present east wall.
West gable, bellcote and two blocked lancets.
Heather thatched until 1733, abandoned 1862,
restored, 1931.

1 South Turnpike, late 18th century
The oldest cottage in the village, with coved
chimneys and bulging rocky plinth, faces the
river lane and has its gable end to the present
1802 high road. This indicates the ancient
dominance of the north/south river crossing.

Two terraces along **North Deeside Road**, built
soon after 1802, form a harmonious unity
enhanced by the 'conservation landscaping' of
the street furniture and discrete cobbled parking
bays. Many attractive minor variations in the
two-storey houses, but they are united by an even
roofline and rhythmic succession of sash
windows. **Tollhouse**, Pitmurchie Road, bow
fronted, marks the west end of the village.

Top *Potarch Hotel*. Above *Potarch Bridge*.

During the construction of **Potarch
Bridge**, *the floating of timber down the Dee
was then much practised, and by the
careless neglect of precautions above
Potarch, where it was the habit to place
single trees on the river bank to await the
first flooding that might occur, a sudden
rising of the river swept a great body of this
timber against the half-built bridge and
nearly destroyed it.*
G M Fraser, *The Old Deeside Road*, 1921

Below *Kincardine O'Neil, south side of
Main Street*. Bottom *Old Parish Church*.

When the railway bypassed Kincardine O'Neil in 1859, and the line was routed through Torphins instead, the 'oldest village in Deeside', recorded since 1228, went into a time warp. It missed out on most Victorian developments and retained the modest and homogenous granite high street which had evolved with the coming of the turnpike in 1802. The parish therefore divides into three sections, the villages of Kincardine O'Neil and Torphins, and the secretive rolling countryside between them which conceals many ambitious houses, amenably located on south-facing slopes and enjoying wide views over the Dee valley.

From top *Episcopal Church; Old Rectory; Canmore Place; Kirkland Lodge*.

Episcopal Church, 1866, William Ramage
Decent compact gothic, rough snecked rubble, with steep roof and attractive decorative woodwork on the lucarnes and porch. Small steeple, good cast-iron cresting and gutter brackets.

Old Rectory, 1863, William Ramage
Cheerful L-shaped house with decorative bargeboards and overhanging eaves, and canted wooden porch in the re-entrant. Bargeboards and *boiserie* porch provide good vernacular detail to **village hall**.

Canmore Place, 1999, Gokay Deveci
A radical new development, grafting a totally modern and alien style to this sensitive site. Green wood cladding and shingle roofs cover single-storey-and-attic blocks of terraced cottages. The aim was to provide affordable housing for locals, using eco-friendly building materials, and the scheme succeeds admirably, partly owing to the attention to layout and detail. Neat paling fences, good garden sheds, common greens, tactful tree planting and parking.

Old Smiddy, mid-19th century
Retains its original hearth and an impressive array of hand-made tools; now a visitor centre.

Gordon Arms Hotel, *c*.1820
For Peter Gordon of Craigmyle. Terminates the north terrace with log-column porch and round-cornered, single-storey addition which echoes the tollhouse at the other end of the village (contrast the generous eaved dormers here with the latter's ungainly extension).

Parish Church, 1860–2, James Matthews
Early English granite box with three shafted lancets and bellcote. Bell by John Mowat, 1744. Uninspired, particularly given the fine carving on the old church opposite, and suffering from the loss of its harling, *c*.1988.

Kirkland Lodge, 1844, J & W Smith
Tudor, L-plan former manse, with round-arched porch in re-entrant. High-quality cut granite and interior woodwork, but mean proportions to rooms. Somewhat forbidding with its plum-coloured harling, 1999. One of the series of the Smiths' manses, including Tough (see *Gordon* in this series) and Tarland.

Norton House, from early 19th century
Twin-bay front and canted *boiserie* porch added
late 19th century, staircase rises from porch to first-
floor entrance. Additions, 1875, William Smith.

Ross Cottage and **Hillhead**, Cochran's Croft,
late 18th/early 19th century
Two-storey, three-bay coursed granite, original
woodwork. A yeoman-like pair of detached
houses, contrasting with the terraces in the heart of
the village. Subtle variations in detail, particularly
the proportion of wall to window, add interest.

West Lodge, Kincardine House, 1897, Niven and
Wigglesworth
Neat vernacular conical turret and crowstepped
gable given crisp Arts & Crafts treatment, with
rustic carved segmental arch over entrance, and
good woodwork.

104 **Kincardine House**, 1897, Niven and Wigglesworth
Two-storey-basement-and-attic, asymmetrical
baronial mansion for Mary and Frank Pickering.
The house has an extravagant flair more
associated with American millionaire dreams than
with pedantic Scottish Baronial. Harled with
carved facings and rugged rocky rustication.
Somewhat overloaded roofline crams in features
from Fyvie and Crathes, while the expanse of
Tudor mullion windows of the south front
squeezes aspects of Hardwick Hall between
Scottish dormers and cap-houses. Baroque front
doorpiece appears borrowed from an Edwardian
Regent Street department store. Exterior is an
overwhelming surprise, rising out of the hillside
like Banff Springs Hotel (Alberta, Canada), but
first impressions deceive. There are only four
rooms on the main floor, great hall, drawing
room, dining room and billiard room (now
kitchen), and perhaps 20 bedrooms. Hall is

Top Ross Cottage. *Middle* West Lodge,
Kincardine House. *Above* Entrance,
Kincardine House. *Left* Kincardine House.

Above East Lodge, Kincardine House.
Right Dess House.

covered in finely detailed Arts & Crafts panelling; drawing room has lightly moulded plasterwork; imposing marble entrance hall is vaulted.

Stables, mainly 1874, James Thomson; south-east part late 18th century. Castellated central tower with good modern wooden porches. **East Lodge**, early 19th century, broad-eaved piend roof supported by columned angle porches; quirky granite eyebrows over windows. A reminder of the two earlier classical houses on the site of Kincardine House, 1780 and 1850.

105 **Dess House**, 1851, Thomas Mackenzie and James Matthews
Well-proportioned baronial mansion for Duncan F and E B Davidson, with all the essential features: cap-house, corbelled turret, crowstepped gables, circular stairturret and four-storey crenellated square tower. Crisp granite ashlar with cable mouldings. East wing burnt down, 1956. Terrazzo over arched gallery with belvedere added to west, 1890s, W R Davidson, architect son of the family and owner of the house. **Lodge**, c.1860, probably James Matthews (of Ardoe House and Glenmillan). Circular turret, heavy granite-faced doorway with bay window above, now harled in ice-cream pink. Details somewhat over emphasised for a house of this size (colour p.72).

Westerton Farmhouse, early 19th century
Single storey with canted dormers, unusual single bay wings with compact piend roofs added shortly afterwards. Interior considerably altered but in keeping with vernacular style.

Craigmyle West Lodge, 1902, Sir Robert Lorimer
Nicely proportioned semicircular stairtower with bell-canted roof and adjacent Dutch gables. Attractive balance between rough granite on the

Craigmyle West Lodge.

tower, harling and carved margins, complemented by the gatepiers with broken pediment and good decorative wrought-iron gates. A similar formula used on his lodge at Pitkerro, 1903–4 (see *Dundee* in this series).

106 Craigmyle, from 1676
Originally a tall compact house with Dutch wallhead gable (as at Frendraught, see *Gordon* in this series) by the Burnetts, cadets of the Crathes family. Extended and modernised, 1902, Sir Robert Lorimer for R P Robertson-Glasgow, who reproduced this theme in his wing, resulting in a rather extended, sprawling plan. Blown up by owner, 1960. Modern 1960s' bungalow incorporates triple-arch loggia and finely carved granite front doorpiece from Lorimer's house.

107 Learney House, *c*.1747
E-plan, two to three storeys (depending on the fall of the ground), coursed rubble with crowstepped gables, with wings facing north; central block reconstructed, 1838, John Smith, after fire damage, with porch to north, south face completely rebuilt and attics added to east wing. South-west corner rebuilt, 1847, probably J and W Smith. North-west wing raised to two storeys, 1868, J Russell Mackenzie, to give present E-shaped plan. Original 18th-century panelling in east wing, 1840s' decoration in dining room. With its many windows and rather plain walls, the house has a somewhat bleak appearance.

Terraces lead past sculptured yews to picturesque **garden house**, *c*.1850, probably J and W Smith, with generous mullion windows in a corbelled timber front and playful bargeboards. **Stableblock** *well contrived and at a proper distance from the house* has rear portion, *c*.1750, main façade with classic pediment John Smith?, 1838. South-west lodge, **Caillie Brae**, early 20th century, rubble tower and coursed rubble rectangular wing, clearly inspired by Craigmyle West Lodge, but

From top Craigmyle, 1902; Craigmyle, 2000; Learney House; stables, Learney House; Caillie Brae.

111

Learney North Lodge.

William Brebner, a businessman, banker and merchant (an Inverness family with property in Aberdeen) built the core of Learney House and the estate, *c*.1747–50. He was renowned for clearing the fields of stones, enclosing them with dykes and starting the extensive tree plantations, draining the land and building excellent accommodation for his tenants. The estate later descended to the Innes family, of whom Sir Thomas Innes, 7th Baron of Learney, was Lord Lyon King of Arms.

managing to look more like a Kentish oast house than a baronial tower. **Invergownie**, gamekeeper's cottage, with Dutch helm roof, ivy-patterned bargeboards and pine log porch (colour p.123).

Mill of Learney, 19th century, two storey coursed granite and eccentrically placed vent, now converted to private house with robust finish and good small-pane windows. **Learney North Lodge**, early 19th century, single storey with canted front and gothic windows, pyramid roof and circular central chimney.

Old Tollhouse, Drumlasie, early 19th century Bow fronted, sympathetic extension, 1990s, balancing rectangular bay and attractive slate pitched roof.

Mill of Ennets, Tornaveen, 19th century, L-shaped with kiln vent. Converted 1990s, skilful pointing and suitable new small-pane windows have resulted in a particularly pleasing external appearance.

TORPHINS

This village, now a bulging cluster of 'executive' commuter homes, began to expand with the arrival of the railway in 1859 (station demolished).

Parish Church (former North Church), 1874–5, J Russell Mackenzie
Coursed granite and slate with polygonal apse at entrance and tower to one side. An imaginative design providing excitement with its soaring Burgundian roofline, extenuated gables and scissors roof truss, showing the influence of Alexander Ellis.

South Church, 1905, George Watt
No-nonsense granite former Free Church with triple lancets and square gothic tower with spirelet. Wagon ceiling on carved open-work corbels; some decorative Art Nouveau glass. Now a furniture shop.

Learney Arms Hotel, early 19th century
Rear wing L-plan with canted entrance bay; front 1874, two storey and attic with small angle tower and crowstepped gable.

Learney Hall, 1899, Jenkins and Marr
Village hall built to celebrate golden wedding of the laird, Thomas Innes; with confident crenellated tower, crowstepped gables and particularly subtle handling of granite, careful shading of tones and textures.

Top *Old Tollhouse*. Middle *Mill of Ennets*. Above *Parish Church*.

Mains of Easter Beltie, 19th century
Steading converted to multiple residences, 1990s.
Thin-frame picture windows below segmental
arches, more successful gable dormers, sheltered
courtyard, good variety and scale, messy
fenestration, concrete tile roof. An unusually high
density complex for an isolated spot.

Pitmurchie House, *c*.1850
Commanding residence with substantial classical
centrepiece and later bow-fronted wings for H J
Barlow, an Aberdeen lawyer; now a nursing home.

LUMPHANAN

Lumphanan is a tucked away parish, not quite
reaching the Dee and not quite reaching the high
hills. Until 1860, when J W Barclay, an Aberdeen
businessman, drained the Loch of Auchlossan,
the low fertile ground was dominated by a
swamp and the small townships clustered
around the higher ground. The kirkton sank into
peaceful obscurity when the railway arrived in
the present village in 1859.

Top *Mains of Easter Beltie*. Above
Pitmurchie House. Left *Old Parish Church
and Manse*.

Kirkton, on its steep hillock above a brook, when
viewed from the east, builds up like a
Burgundian apse, with the low manse offices
leading to the sprawling façades of the manse,
topped by the sober box and bellcote of the **Old
Parish Church**, 1762, rubble box with square-
headed windows. Interior gutted, now a studio.

Lumphanan was notorious around 1600
for witch trials. The activities took place
by the *gryt stane of Craigleuch*, on the
north side of the hill. The warlock
controlling the coven was Colin Massie
of Gledye. Isobel Ritchie was tried for
being the Devil's special servant and
domestic, as attested by her
participation in two devilish dances
between Lumphanan and Craiglash.
The most outrageous charge was
against Margaret Clark, summoned to
help a cow whose calf would not suck at
Mill of Auchlossan. *By thy devilische
socerie and inchantment, efter thow had
sitten downe in the staw, before the cowis
heid, thou gaue ane devilische low and
terible voice, quhairthrow the hail houss
trimlit and schuik, and immediatelie the cow
tuik the calff; and throw the terrible cry
gyven* [by you] *the wyff of the said
Alexander being exceidinglie affryit and
terrifiet, tuik immediatelie and deadlie
sickness by thy socerie.* Most witches were
taken to Aberdeen for burning, one of
them so frail and old that she had to be
taken in a wheelbarrow. Some were
executed locally at Gallows Cairn,
Craigour, east of Torphins. Craiglash
Hill now supplies the Council with
crushed grey granite for road works.

108 **Old Manse**, *c*.17th century
Core of this irregular plan is a long, narrow
building, running east/west, with walls over 1m
thick; bulging rocky plinth; low-ceilinged ground
floor, higher ceilings upstairs, with evidence of a
modified attic floor. Features suggest an original
structure like nearby Mains of Auchlossan.
Modified 1782; sitting room and kitchen
extensions 1828 and 1869 by George Spark and
James Thomson.

At **Auchlossan**, the armorial plaque belongs to the Rose family who held the estate from 1363–1709 when Captain Francis Rose was killed at the battle of Malplaquet.

Right Mains of Auchlossan. *Below* Peel of Lumphanan.

Contrary to Shakespeare's denouement at Dunsinane, ancient sources place the murder of Macbeth at Lumphanan. *Macbeth seeing his own forces daily diminishing, and those of his adversary increasing, suddenly left the southern parts of his kingdom, and fled to the north, in whose narrow passes, and in the depths of whose forests, he hoped to find safety. Malcolm, however, quickly followed him across the mountains to Lunfanan, where he slew him, in a skirmish with his followers in 1056.*
Forduni, *Scotichronicon*

109 Mains of Auchlossan, late 17th century
Narrow five bay, two storey and garret, Auchlossan looks like a badly harled barrack, brutally 'modernised', interior stripped 19th century, but its details are rewarding. Four shot holes by front door; remains of bar holes can be seen in lower windows. Heraldic plaque, removed from its frame above front door, re-used in croft. Row of corbels projects at eaves level to north (rear), possibly for tying down a thatch roof; one fine fireplace with bolection mouldings survives inside; re-used lintel/fireplace forms kitchen windowsill.

The Durward family were given the lands at Lumphanan by the king, *c.*1228, and constructed the motte. Edward I visited the castle in 1296. The Haa-ton House was derelict by the 1780s.

Stothert Memorial Church.

110 Peel of Lumphanan, 13th century
Motte, *c.*40m x 50m wide and 10m high; ditch and encircling bank. An unusually impressive earthwork, locally comparable to the Doune of Invernochty at Strathdon and The Bass at Inverurie (see *Gordon* in this series). On its summit, foundations of 15th-century **Haa-ton House**, hall house, *c.*16m x 3m. Supposedly marking the site of Macbeth's death is **Macbeth's Cairn**, a pile of stones over 40m in circumference.

Stothert Memorial Church (former Free Church), 1870, W Henderson and Son
Slim west tower and steeple emphasise the verticality of this prominent and elevated site. Plain gothic harled nave, splendid early medieval **font**, a rough boulder bowl 3m in circumference, moved from the old parish church to this site (see also Tullich p.141).

Macbeth Arms Hotel and **Lumphanan Stores**, 1860, John Stuart
Symbolising the progress of the railway, traditional two storey, three bay, harled; shop's four distinctive arches make a fine entrance.

Findrack House, from *c*.1700
Rolls out like a long carpet, each section in a new style unrelated to the previous. Rear (north) wing was plain rectangular farmhouse, *c*.1700; east wing, 1862, William Smith, a mixture of baronial tower and gables with classical entrance; south wing originally 19th century with canted granite bay at each end; south-west bay opened up, 1980s, by William Cowie, into spectacular glass fronted, split-level sun rooms. The glass addition, although unbalancing, throws the house out into its magnificent terraced gardens and view over the Dee valley (colour p.123). Old **walled garden** with finialed circular doocot and baluster sundial of 1846 for Adam Charles.

Glenmillan House, 1872, James Matthews
L-plan with circular balustraded entrance tower, the serious baronial dressings (Ardoe House in miniature, see p.76) suggest a gigantic mansion for the Lord Provost of Aberdeen, but with the loss of the east wing in 1940s' fire, the house only has three formal rooms and a few bedrooms. Some fine 18th-century marble fireplaces. Small upstairs living room, with high ceiling and elongated windows, takes advantage of the view. Stained glass on the staircase commemorates Dr James Mackie, a psychiatrist with strong interests in Scottish history. Re-used date stone on stable block: *FR/BF 1688*.

Top *Findrack House*. Above *Glenmillan House*. Below *Aboyne Castle, 2000*. Left *Aboyne Castle, 1968*.

ABOYNE

111 **Aboyne Castle**, from early 17th century
Originally square plan, five storey, corbelled out at the top, with ogee-roofed cap-house and probably with classical balustrade. Enhanced, 1671, by Charles Gordon, 1st Earl of Aboyne, and his wife Elizabeth Lyon, with their strong Catholic allegiance emphasised by *IHS* and Instruments of the Passion inscribed on the dated door lintel.

This community began at old Aboyne church, east of the village by Formaston. The present settlement, Charleston of Aboyne, was established by royal charter in 1676, the creation of Charles Gordon, the 1st Earl. A handsome and spacious village, unusual in this district because it centres on the extensive green, giving a somewhat English impression, enhanced by the leafy Home Counties' arrangement of housing, surrounded by generous gardens and deciduous trees (colour p.122). Although the castle, church and two inns were here before the arrival of the railway in 1859, the remainder of the village developed after that date, particularly as a summer and commuter resort for Aberdeen.

George, the 5th Earl of Aboyne, *danced with Marie Antoinette and danced away his fortune. He was an old Beau of the Regency, carefully dressed to the last and a great deal made up, the blue-blackness of his hair or wig impressing me very much* (John Bulloch, *The Earls of Aboyne*). During his lifetime, the estate was sequestered in the 1850s.

George Truefitt, 1842–1902, a pupil of Lewis Cottingham, developed as a High Victorian rogue architect building both churches and public building with an idiosyncratic style, latterly in the Arts & Crafts mode: Manchester Royal Exchange Assurance offices, 1868; St George's, Tufnell Park, 1868. He designed Cunliffe Brooks' bank in Manchester in 1867.

Coo Cathedral.

East wing added to create a symmetrical façade, 1801, five bays including two flanking towers, on either side of a half-round central bay. Worked on by William Burn, 1835, James Matthews, 1860, and George Truefitt, 1890s, when the castle was owned by Sir William Cunliffe Brooks.

Drastically reduced and recreated, 1975, by Ian Begg. Old core, with some reconstruction, has emerged as a compact and practical family home. Kitchen and dining room in vaulted basement; modern Jacobean plaster ceiling in sitting room and library above. Spiral stairs made of concrete, plus a lift, vaults made of mesh and plaster. Square cap-house, wooden platform balcony. Walled courtyard has open-topped turrets like Muchalls.

Geddes

112 Coo Cathedral, Mains of Aboyne, 1889
Part of the model farm by George Truefitt for Sir William Cunliffe Brooks. Exterior dominated by four fanlight archways, large hip roof and two lower matching side wings. Basilican interior, surreal for a cowshed, has Romanesque arcades of dressed stone forming nave and aisles.

Below *Aboyne Parish Church*.
Bottom *Aboyne Business Centre*.

Geddes

East Lodge, Aboyne Castle, 1896
Substantial house featuring bold tower and conical roof. Fine granite detailing of rope mouldings and heraldic plaque. Similar **West Lodge**, 1890s, by George Truefitt.

113 Aboyne Parish Church, 1842, John Smith
Moved from Formaston to the green in 1707. Perpendicular gothic, east front has bold buttresses and pinnacles, bellcote and traceried window. Interior, plain woodwork, orientated south. Similar to Keig (see *Gordon* in this series). Incorporates 1761 Huntly vault.

Aboyne Business Centre, 1875
Originally the school, it complements the adjacent church with its sturdy sequence of four gables and generous roofs; extended 1890, 1901. Tall stone steeple of former **Free Church**, 1869,

J Russell Mackenzie, now community hall and Masonic Lodge, gives more character and focus to the green than the parish church.

Huntly Arms.

Alexander Marshall Mackenzie, 1848–1933, from Elgin, was trained by James Matthews and David Bryce. A founder member of the Aberdeen Ecclesiological Society, he demonstrated a flair for medieval buildings, demonstrated by numerous churches including Craigiebuckler and Powis in Aberdeen, and the enlargement of Marischal College in 1906. Crathie contains elements from his previous medieval churches. His work at Elphinstone Hall and New Kings, Aberdeen University, provided inspiration for Aboyne Victory Hall. He also designed the monumental and classical Aberdeen Art Gallery, Cowdray Hall and South United Free Church. The Aberdeen Capitol Cinema is in Art Deco style. From his London offices, with his son Alec, he designed the Waldorf Hotel, 1906, with its revolutionary steel skeleton. He moved out to Coull, building Coull House for himself and excavating the castle.

Below *Aboyne Station.* Middle *Aboyne Victory Hall.* Bottom *St Thomas Episcopal Church.*

114 **Huntly Arms**, from late 18th century
Making a decent laird's inn, the central five bays of this H-plan have 12-pane sashes, coved chimney tops, raised margins. Central porch and two projecting side wings added, late 19th century. Core of south wing was an independent façade, two storeys and dormers, later heightened to its present square crenellated appearance. Some good late 18th-century woodwork inside. Forlorn polygonal **gazebo**, mid-19th century, has decorative slates depicting card suits, reflecting the gambling sessions held there. A rare garden building for a hotel, its decaying outline now mocked by new supermarket below.

115 **Aboyne Station**, 1889
Undoubtedly the boldest style-statement on the Royal Deeside Line, possibly the result of Sir William Cunliffe Brooks monopolising the development of Aboyne at this date. Sprightly conical towers flank the ticket-office area. Excellent detailing of well-cut stone, window margins, corbels. Railway arrived here in 1859, station closed 1966, now well restored as retail units.

116 **Aboyne Victory Hall**, 1921,
A Marshall Mackenzie
Noble village hall with fine stonework and a high roof. Three grey ashlar arches across entrance, glazed and traceried Remembrance Apse, inspired by Mackenzie's oriel at new King's College, 1912 (see *Aberdeen* in this series). Fine open rafter interior with towering beams.

117 **St Thomas Episcopal Church**, 1909,
Fryers and Penman
Gifted by George Coats, 1st Baron Glentanar, based on Burrough Church, Leicester, where the baron had his estate. Gothic, nave and aisles, stone steeple, 16th- and 17th-century Flemish stained glass. Another taste of England in Aboyne.

Top *Boat Inn.* Right *Bridgend Cottage.*

Boat Inn, Charleston Road
Was one long thatched house, consisting of dwelling house, byre and stables, modernised, *c.*1880s, by Mr Sandison. From the days of Bonty Ferry, before the Earl of Aboyne began the first bridge in 1828.

Below *The Glebe.* Middle *Ladywood Lodge.* Bottom *Rhu-na-haven.*

118 **Bridgend Cottage**, Bridgeview Road, *c.*1830
A miniature classic, definitely perjink, tollhouse for the Earl of Aboyne's suspension bridge of 1831. Finely cut rusticated ashlar; segmental arches over windows and door, fanlight, oversailing roof, neoclassical iron railings. Along with Park, one of the best classical designs on Deeside.

The Glebe, Bridgeview Road, from 1790
Narrow three-storey old wing, with moulded skewputts, thick walls, coved chimneys and granite staircase up to first floor. Two-storey addition, 1835, mars the integrity of the entrance façade.

Ladywood Lodge, Bridgeview Road, 1904, George Bennett Mitchell
Dower house for Lady Jane Cunliffe Brooks. Rough ashlar with thick joints, below fluted half-timbering and reeded bargeboards. Good Arts & Crafts interior with leaded lights, fine woodwork and some tiling. A pacy screen of windows rattles across the garden front, and the whole house gains a relaxed air with pine-pole verandas and canopied entrance walk. Although an Aberdonian, Mitchell introduced much Surrey half-timbering to this area.

119 **Rhu-na-haven**, Rhu-na-haven Road, 1907, wings 1911–12, Sir Robert Lorimer
Displays undoubted quality but lacks flair and excitement, perhaps because it is Lorimer's only house made of granite. Facing the river, a

symmetrical façade of two bays on either side of a
central bow, dormers with Dutch-gable pediments.
Rather mundane, considering its splendid aspect.
Entrance face broken up with twin-arched porch,
crowstepped gable, stone-flagged hip roofs.
Excellent panelling, plasterwork and tiles inside.
For J Herbert Taylor, tea planter.

120 **North Balnagowan**, 1977, Alistair Urquhart
Traditional steading by the master stonemason of
Aboyne Castle (and elsewhere), for himself.
Dormers penetrate the roofline with a variety of
carved pediments; his initials, those of his wife
Mary, and the tools of his trade. Bow-fronted
extension to living room; forestair to loft;
coursed granite boulders, unharled. Ruggedly
innovative vernacular.

121 The poorhouses at **Craigwell**, 19th century, a
reminder of the original parish centre at nearby
Formaston. Two humble rows of eight and four
dwellings in long narrow terraces, now knocked
into larger cottages.

Top *Entrance, Rhu-na-haven.*
Above *North Balnagowan.*

SOUTH DEESIDE ROAD:
GLEN TANAR TO ABERGELDIE
Over the bridge at Aboyne, the pleasant South
Deeside Road (B976) bypasses all villages, with
diversions up Glen Tanar and Glenmuick, ending
beyond Abergeldie at Balmoral, finally branching
off to the lonely crags of Loch Muick. The first
diversion is up Glen Tanar, with its sparkling
river leaping over fractured pink granite. It
contains an impressive remnant of the
Caledonian pine forest. The lost settlement at
Braeloine (near car park) supplied travellers over
the Firmounth drove road. Today the glen reflects
the extraordinary vision and passion of Sir
William Cunliffe Brooks.

Below *Poorhouses, Craigwell.* Middle
Summerhouse, Queen's Loch. Bottom
Auchintoul.

122 **Summerhouse**, Queen's Loch, *c.*1930
The ultimate use of *boiserie* and bark. Entire hut
faced with split logs, gutters and down pipes
disguised in bark; porch columns are forked tree
trunks supporting the gutter. A woodland
design that belongs to its setting and retains a
leisure mood.

Auchintoul, South Deeside, 1893, ?G B Mitchell
Swiss chalet-style summerhouse, tongue and
groove lined, sensibly extended, 1998, by Jenkins
and Marr, with a well-lit tower keeping the same
style but at last maximising the magnificent
location over the river.

Craigendinnie.

Sir William Cunliffe Brooks, a Manchester banker, *the apparently irascible old martinet*, bought the Glen Tanar estate in 1869. His daughter Amy married Charles Gordon, 11th Marquis of Huntly, in 1869, and in 1888 Brooks bought Aboyne Castle, which resulted in a strong Glen Tanar influence on the appearance of Aboyne.

Below *Ballroom, Glen Tanar House.* Middle *Glen Tanar House, 1975.* Bottom *Glen Tanar House, 2000.*

123 **Craigendinnie**, from 1894
Sturdy Jacobean, rough-hewn granite bound together by roving stringcourse. Most conventional house on Glen Tanar estate, extended, 1918, as dower house for Margaret, Lady Glentanar.

GLEN TANAR
124 **Glen Tanar House**, 1890s, George Truefitt
Originally looked as extensive as a sprawling village, partly two storey, partly single storey and dormers with vast areas of disjointed sweeping slate roof, windows were long ribbons of Tudor mullion and transoms. Each façade was an exercise in asymmetry and quirky detail: a little tower, bays, bows, rugged granite chimneys at all angles, pine pillar porches. In 1906 Fryers and Penman added more complex details: stone-faced entrance tower, pediment dormers. *It has risen from a shooting box to a large two-winged mansion adorned with rustic work, stained glass, pine dados, panelled ceilings and antique furnishings.* Only the ballroom survives, with round oast-like tower at one end, two Venetian windows and elegant fish-scale slates. Inside, open timber roof covered in stags' heads.
Demolished and rebuilt 1975, by Sir James Dunbar-Nasmith for Jean Bruce.

Much-reduced single-storey new house retains a flavour of the old, L-plan, dormers, steep slate roof. In place of Truefitt's refined stone detailing, there are harling, concrete sills and picture windows, to comply with planning permission. The house has always been the least satisfactory part of this exquisite estate.

RCAHMS

Geddes

Jonathan Smith

Geddes

Top left *Music room, Crathes Castle.* Top right *Doocot, Crathes Castle.* Above *Gazebo, Crathes Castle.* Left *Crathes Castle.* Below *Birkwood, Banchory.*

Geddes

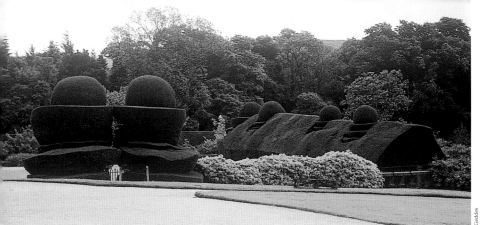

Geddes

Geddes

Geddes

Top *Garden, Crathes Castle.* Above
Bridges, Milton of Crathes. Right *The
Green, Aboyne.* Below *'The sun peeped o'er
yon southland hills' by Joseph Farquharson.*

Aberdeen Art Gallery

122

Top *Braemar Highland Gathering*. Middle
Invergownie, Torphins. Left *Bucket Mill,
Birse*. Above *Findrack House, Lumphanan*.

123

Top *Cambus o' May Bridge.* Above
Butcher's shop, Braemar. Right *Elizabeth
Cottage, Banchory.*

124

Jim Henderson

Geddes

Geddes

Geddes

Top *Potarch Bridge*. Middle *Glen o' Dee Hospital, Banchory.* Above *Cambus o' May Station.* Left *Burnroot steading wall, Aboyne.*

125

Top *Linn of Dee Bridge.* Above *Linn of Dee.*

Top left *Balmoral from west.* Above
Garbh-allt-shiel bridge. Left *The Square,
Tarland.* Below *Knock Castle.*

127

Top *Mar Lodge*. Right *Auchendryne Jubilee Hall, Braemar*. Above *Royal picnic cottage, Linn of Quoich*. Below *Fraser's Bridge, Clunie water*.

Geddes

5 Bush Cottages.

Sir William Cunliffe Brooks employed an English team to create his Glen Tanar estate: Thomas Mawson, the landscape architect; Daniel Gibson, Mawson's architectural partner; and George Truefitt of Worthing, working throughout the 1890s. The result is highly original, Arts & Crafts, Art Nouveau, showing an outstanding appreciation for the rugged local building materials (pink granite and pine).

5 Bush Cottages, *c.*1885, George Truefitt
Turret with conical roof and decorative slates, a circle of arched windows forming belvedere, stained glass, cherrycocking, crowstepped gables. A cottage for Rapunzel, completing the complex of keepers' and kennel buildings ('the keepers' palaces', *if the canine inmates are not comfortable and grateful, they ought to be*). Throughout the estate, the drystone walling and little bridges *I believe to be the finest in Great Britain, a fact on which my client greatly prided himself* (T H Mawson). **Stableblock** retains the single-storey-and-dormer scheme of the old main house, but more relaxed and loosely laid out.

Greystone Cottage, George Truefitt
Brilliant exercise on the square box bungalow. Recessed porch of pine trunks, pyramid roof with patterned slates and V-fronted swept dormer, like a pointed eyebrow.

125 **Chapel of St Lesmo**, Braeloine, 1872, George Truefitt
Alone in the meadow, incorporating arch fragments of 17th-century Braeloine House, coursed granite and slate, with a turf roof western extension. Pews lined with deerskin. Cunliffe Brooks' gravestone in churchyard, based on design of Kinord Pictish cross (see p.140).

Bridge of Tanar, late 18th century
Segmental arch, humpbacked; picturesque location among fine trees, linking the Firmounth drove road to the Dee.

126 **Bridge of Ess**, 1894
Stone bridge with cast-iron crested parapet forms a bold introduction to the estate. Re-used voussoir dated 1779. **Lodge**, 1890s, probably George Truefitt, entrance landscape Thomas Mawson. Square tower of four storeys, black basecourses, pink above, cream quoins. Solid corbelled parapet. A dream honeymoon retreat perched above a fine rock pool.

From top *Greystone Cottage; Chapel of St Lesmo; Bridge of Tanar; Bridge of Ess and lodge.*

Geddes

Geddes

Geddes

Geddes

Above *Drinking trough*.
Right *Fasnadarach*.

In addition to the buildings on Glen Tanar estate, Sir William Cunliffe Brooks embellished his glen with homilies carved on wells and wayside stones: *The worm of the still is the deadliest snake on the hill; Well to know that you are well off; Honest water never left man in the mire; Drink, Thank, Think.* Tirelessly energetic, he rose each day at 7 am *to the piper's wail.* Finding him at work one morning at 6, Lord Swansea commented *'I wouldn't have your job for ten thousand year'. 'Neither would I',* replied Brooks. He employed 250 masons continually for 11 years. His promotion of English Arts & Crafts made a profound impact on the locality: *He failed to appreciate that Scotland possessed any architectural tradition for he immediately set about eliminating everything which appeared incongruous to his English eyes* (Fenton Wyness, *Royal Valley*).

In 1905 the estate was bought by George Coats, later Lord Glentanar, the thread manufacturer from Paisley and is still owned by his family. He continued the energetic building tradition, contributing the Victory Hall and St Thomas' Church, Aboyne.

SOUTH DEESIDE
Glen Tanar School, George Truefitt
Two square blocks with steep conical roofs and louvres, like Kentish oast houses. Nearby, **drinking trough**, 1897, for Queen Victoria's jubilee. Beside the well-dressed wall is a recess containing a rough boulder with a Brooks homily: *Shape thyself for use. The stone that may fit in the wall is not left in the way.* This philosophy is epitomised by the steading at **Burnroot**, 1893, where Aberdeen bond is used to show off the exquisite jewel-like quality of Glen Tanar building stone, pink, blue, black, white, golden (colour p.125).

127 **Fasnadarach**, 1896, A Marshall Mackenzie
Elegant Voysey-like fishing lodge for Sir Ian Cecil, a cousin of Brooks. Complex entrance front of sweeping roofs and gables conceals the real purpose of the house: a superb sequence of rooms on two floors, virtually perched over the riverbank. Interior details complete, including good Art Nouveau door furniture.

Deecastle
An over-dramatic name for an old settlement site. Hunting lodge of the Earl of Aboyne on the hillock in the 16th century; foundations beneath the present 'chapel house' may be the Earls' tutor's house from 1703–6. Present three-bay, two-storey house was latterly the Free Church, 1843, and now a private house. Of greater interest, the **steading**, perhaps early 17th century, drystone, with rough monolith lintels, originally thatched.

Steading, Deecastle.

The pleasant castle of Kean-na-Kyll (Deecastle) was built some few years ago by the Marquis of Huntly at a delightful retreat shaded on all sides by woods, in a situation highly suitable for fishing, fowling and the hunting of stags and does.
Sir Robert Gordon of Straloch, 1662, *Macfarlane's Collections*, 1907

Birkelunn, 1938
Given by Thor Thoreson of Oslo to his daughter Grete Dagbjørt, wife of Thomas Baron Glentanar, this fully functioning Norwegian hytte is a log cabin with grass roof. Raised foundations of local rock, grass and flowers on roof blend into the meadow and walls merge into the forest. Mighty

roof timbers from Trondelag. Although alien, in the appropriate setting this type of well-insulated 'natural' house has many advantages over the local flat-pack kit homes.

Above Birkelunn. Left Pannanich Hotel.

The healing properties of **Pannanich Wells** were discovered around 1760 by a scrofulous woman who was guided there by a dream. Their mineral content still provides respite for ailments like arthritis. The spa was developed by Col Francis Farquharson who *erected several houses on the spot for water drinkers, a public and private bath, an octagon for the better sort to retire to.*
Statistical Account, 1791–9

*I've seen the auld seem young and frisky
Without the aid of ale or whisky
I've seen the dullest hearts grow frisky
At blithesome, healthful Pannanich.*
John Ogilvy, 19th century

128 **Pannanich Hotel** and **Wells**, from 1770
The springs issue from a deep geological fault which runs across the Dee and is particularly visible as a cleft on the hilltop opposite. The **well heads**, *c.*1770, are encased in stone: upper has pediment above a recess; lower has stepped top and seat. Water is now extracted at a modern bottling plant below the road. The hotel perches on the steep hillside, just east of the springs, two long parallel rows of accommodation; upper two storey, rubble; lower with bowed central bay and four bays to each side. Owing to the slope of the hill, the wallhead is higher at the back than the front.

House of Glenmuick, 1870,
Sir Samuel Morton Peto (demolished 1947)
Vast house for Sir James Mackenzie, Aberdeen silk merchant in India, formed three sides of a square, nine bays long on the sides, dominated by a 25m water tower over the *porte-cochère*. The main façade had bay windows in the gable-end bays and at centre.

129 **House of Glenmuick** (former Braickley House), 1898, Daniel Gibson
Dower house to House of Glenmuick and took its name when the main building was demolished. For Sir Alan Mackenzie. Enlarged from a small farmhouse, this is also vast and rambling: basically Tudor, ribbons of large red sandstone mullion windows set in walls of dressed grey granite. South-east wing, 1912, retains style but employs hipped roof. Landscape terraces by T H Mawson command splendid view over Glen Gairn.

*Below House of Glenmuick, pre 1947.
Bottom House of Glenmuick/Braickley House, 2000.*

Above *Mill of Sterin*. Right *Birkhall*.

England! Thy beauties are tame and domestic
To one who has roved o'er the mountains afar:
 O for the crags that are wild and majestic!
The steep frowning glories of wild Lochnagar!
Lord Byron, who spent formative
holidays at Ballaterach (South Deeside),
1795–1803

Glass-alt-Shiel looked so cheerful and comfortable, all lit up and the rooms so cosy and nice. There is a wonderful deal of room in the compact little house … I thought of my darling husband who always wished to build here, in this favourite wild spot, quite in amidst the hills. It is far better to have built a totally new house; but then the sad thought struck me that it was the first Widow's House.
Queen Victoria's Journal

Glass-alt-Shiel, 1895.

GLENMUICK
130 **Mill of Sterin**, mid-19th century
Single storey, characterful dormers, with roofs like pagodas, supported by wooden consoles and topped by finials.

Birkhall, from 1715
Surely the cosiest of the royal homes, set on a sheltered promontory overlooking a neat vegetable garden beside the Muick River, modestly bowered in old roses, the favourite flowers of the Queen Mother.
 Original no-nonsense rectangular east block, five bays, slim with steep roof. Bolection moulded door piece, 1715, with initials of Charles Gordon of Abergeldie. Arms of the Queen Mother in the moulded frame above the door, harled margins to windows. North (entrance) wing, 1880–90, with later tree trunk portico. Conversion and south wing, c.1955, A Graham Henderson, eschews rectilinear classicism of the old block with ogee turret and bow-fronted drawing room.
 Built by Charles Gordon in 1715, Birkhall estate was bought by Prince Albert, 1848, for Prince Edward who did not like it. The house was subsequently let to Lord Glenesk but it is now the residence of the Queen Mother. Mr Gordon's garden *produces as early, and well flavoured fruit as any in the North of Scotland; apples, pears, plumbs, cherries, gooseberries. He has not lost sight of neatness and elegance; he has cleared away the rubbish of nature round his villa, and displayed her beauties to the best advantage* (*Statistical Account*, 1791–9).
 Lodges around the Balmoral estate, often visually gaunt and plain, are infused with Queen Victoria's enthusiasm and pleasure. In the awesome setting of Loch Muick, under the shadow of Lochnagar, **Glass-alt-Shiel**, 1862, twin gables and bow windows, faced the loch below the waterfalls. Replaced a two-room croft.

Allt-na-guibhsaich, 1849, with later alterations
Two crofts: *We have a charming little dining-room, sitting-room, bed-room and dressing-room, all en suite. Our rooms are delightfully papered, the ceilings as well as walls, and very nicely furnished. The silence and solitude, only interrupted by the waving of fir trees, were very solemn and striking (Queen Victoria's Journal, 1849).*

SOUTH DEESIDE

131 **Knock Castle**, early 17th century
A tragic Gordon stronghold. Compact rectangular plan, three storey and attic. Angle turrets have key pattern corbelling like Birse Castle, square cap-house, crowstepped gable, foundations of courtyard enclosure visible. A prominent sentinel to the entrance of Glenmuick (colour p.127).

Knock Cottages, late 19th century
Picturesque group of estate cottages, with ogee timbering on the porches, set back in long cottage gardens.

132 **Abergeldie Castle**, late 16th century
Oblong tower, recognisable by its square topped corner turret capped by ogee-roofed belfry and later insertion of a Venetian window dormer, newly pink harled. Vaulted kitchen in basement, hall above. A Gordon castle since 1482, rented by the royal family during the later 19th century. Early 19th-century extensions by James Henderson now removed.

THE HOWE OF CROMAR
The parishes of Coull, Tarland and Logie-Coldstone all tumble into a great bowl in the mountains, the Howe of Cromar. This sheltered circle of land is shaped by the mighty flanks of Morven, Pressendye, Craiglich, Mortlich and Craig Dubh, best seen from The Queen's View on

There was a long lasting feud between the Forbes's of Strathgirnock and the Gordons of Knock. In the early 17th century, a Gordon son and Forbes daughter were about to marry against their parents' wishes. Alexander Forbes killed the Gordon suitor and, fearing reprisals, slaughtered the remaining seven sons of Henry Gordon while they were out cutting peat. He left their heads on their peat spades. Hearing the news from the top of his spiral staircase, Henry Gordon swooned and broke his neck falling down the stairs. Alexander Forbes was hanged by a Gordon posse from his own roof tree at Strathgirnock.

Top *Knock Castle*. Middle *Knock Cottages*. Left *Abergeldie Castle, pre demolition 1969*. Above *Abergeldie Castle, 2000*.

the B9119 where wild Lochnagar completes the horizon. It contains the lochs Kinord and Davan and, before drainage in 1830, a large loch spread from Coull to Tarland. Such a favoured landscape has resulted in particularly rich prehistoric remains, focused on the 'navel' of the Howe at Tomnaverie stone circle.

COULL
Coull is exactly what its Gaelic name means, a 'corner or retiring part of the country', tucked into the south-east section of Cromar. Its original significance lay in the old church of St Nathalan, beside the ancient lake shore, and the old track which winds over dry ground north from the Dee towards Alford, via the upland part of the parish at Corse, past the two strategically placed castles of Coull and Corse.

Coull Castle.

Coull Castle was probably built by the Bissetts *c.*1220; it was handed over to the English in 1291 and destroyed by Robert the Bruce's forces in 1308.

Geddes

133 **Coull Castle**, early 13th century
In its day, this must have been one of the great castles of Scotland. Its *enceinte* design is reminiscent of Kildrummy (see *Gordon* in this series) and indeed the carved sandstone facings are transported from the Kildrummy quarry. Curtain-wall with six towers, including two flanking towers at gate and massive donjon with battered foundations in south-west corner. Domestic buildings flanked the stream. Destroyed during a siege (during which the garderobe shafts were blocked solid), early 14th century; excavated 1923, by Douglas Simpson. The crumbling ruin demonstrates the folly of enthusiastic excavation without consolidation.

Parish Church.

Geddes

Parish Church, 1798
Founded by the 7th-century St Nathalan, first recorded in the 12th century belonging to Arbroath Abbey. Present oblong box re-uses the birdcage belfry and 1642 Burgerhuys bell. Interior refurnished in pitch pine, 1925. Mort house in churchyard.

Kirklands of Coull, 1832

Two-storey old manse, well-proportioned three-bay façade with original windows; harled with granite margins. Bee bole in walled 18th-century garden. Elegant semicircular stairturret and fine interior woodwork links it to Drumoak manse by John Smith, Corrachree (Tarland) and to **Wester Coull**, 1840s, a dignified farmhouse, single-storey version of the manse, having the rounded stairturret merely leading to the attic.

Above *Kirklands of Coull.* Left *Coull House.*

Coull House, 1912–14, A Marshall Mackenzie

Stripped Edwardian vernacular house, built by the architect for himself. Three central bays, projecting hip-roofed bays at each end with round-topped windows and balconies. Colonnade loggia across front. A relaxed family style selected by the dramatic architect of Marischal College (see *Aberdeen* in this series).

Greenhill, Gellan, 19th century

An estate cottage of Aboyne Castle, perhaps used as a rehearsal for greater works at the castle, having one tiny ceiling lavishly plastered with free-form vine scrolls.

Below *Greenhill, Gellan.* Bottom *Corse Castle.*

134 Corse Castle, 1581

Ruined, but standing up to the wallhead. Four-storey, Z-plan, rectangular block for William Forbes of Corse, with square tower at one end and round tower at the other. Stairturret in re-entrant and angle turrets on corbels. Vaulted cellar. Carved diamond gunloops, date over door, two framed settings for armorials. A decent candidate for restoration and conversion, discretely situated above its own lake.

William Forbes, whose previous house had been plundered by brigands vowed: *If God spares my life I shall build a house at which thieves shall knock ere they enter.* William's one son became Bishop Patrick Forbes of Aberdeen (1564–1635), and the other 'Danzig Willie' completed Craigievar Castle (see *Gordon* in this series).

House of Corse, 1863, Alexander Ellis and James Giles RA

Surprising Italianate summerhouse for James Ochoncar Forbes of Craigievar, optimistically hoping for sunnier climes. White harled with

granite details; low pitched roof with oversailing eaves; entrance through canted porch; three-storey campanile-style tower with variety of windows; ground floor has round-topped windows, rectangular windows above; canted carved granite bay with balustrade above to south. Varied and stimulating elevations. Inside, Corinthian columns and entablature in galleried hall.

TARLAND
135 **Tomnaverie recumbent stone circle**, *c.*2500–1500 BC
Dominates the parish on its rocky knoll (later used as a quarry for the village) in the centre of the howe. The recumbent and its two flankers majestically frame Lochnagar and the Pass of Ballater, a numinous vista in many conditions of sun and moonlight. Excavations in 2000 have revealed a central cremation area, a platform of smaller stones and, around the edge, a well-formed kerb and the prominent circle of megaliths. A sequence of cupmarks, carved into the living rock, indicates the approach to this sacred area.

From the green stance in **Tarland** it is still possible to visualise the small settlement clustered around its once-prosperous livestock markets.

Myrtlebank, Melgum Road, early 19th century Typifies the older type of single-storey, two-window cottage, once roofed with heather but now with corrugated iron. **Boig Farm**, 18th century, remarkably preserves its 24-pane windows although the interior is gutted.

Old Parish Church, 1762
Roofless, coursed granite; six arched south windows have tripartite keystones. Its glory is the playful bellcote, one of the finest of this local speciality, its rich mouldings topped with elaborate finials.

St Moluag's Parish Church, 1870, William Smith Strong gothic west front with triple arches at entrance and Chartres rose window, 1909, above. Powerful verticality enhanced by buttresses and asymmetry of bellcote and broach spire, 1889–90.

From top House of Corse; Boig Farm; St Moluag's Parish Church; Kirklands of Tarland.

Kirklands of Tarland, 1846,
John and William Smith
L-plan Tudor former manse, with porch in angle, mullion and transom windows. Well-preserved interiors, like Kincardine O'Neil manse (see p.108).

Alastrean House (former Cromar House), c.1903–4, A G Sydney Mitchell
Autumn hunting lodge for the Marquis of Aberdeen. Pink granite ashlar block with hipped roof; garden front nine bays and four turrets; entrance flanked by twin turrets. Interior refitted after 1958 fire. Timeless design with little period detail but significant aspect facing Tomnaverie hill.

Tarland Square, sleepy and dignified, features the **MacRobert Memorial Hall**, 1951, modern-looking ashlar granite, a gift for the benefit of the villagers (colour p.127).

Aberdeen Arms Hotel, 18th century
Three bays, two storeys, coursed granite, *commodious and well frequented*, commands the corner of the road and view to the bridge. Scrolled skewputts are similar to finials on church bellcote and skews on Tillychardoch.

Bridge on **Whiteley Road**, 1824, heralds first stage towards draining the great lake to east of village, 1840. Prominent makers' marks on voussoirs show that a considerable team of masons were working in Tarland in the 1820s.

Tillychardoch, 18th century
T-plan, bulging foundation course, spiral skews, upper windows possibly lengthened, chamfered jambs. Imposing farmhouse by Tarland builders.

136 **Culsh Souterrain**
Well-preserved stone-lined tunnel from an Iron Age settlement, around 2000 years old, leading to underground store. Re-used cupmarked stone in wall testifies to the antiquity of the site.

Corrachree, 1842, James Henderson
Imposing, two-storey house for Lt Col John Farquharson of the East India Company, harled,

Cromar House was built for the Marquis and Marchioness of Aberdeen, John Hamilton-Gordon, 1847–1943, and Ishbel Marjoribanks, known as 'We Twa', to provide a retreat from Haddo (see *Gordon* in this series). As Governor-General of Canada, 1893–8, John presided over the opening up of the Wild West, with many Rocky Mountains bearing Aberdeenshire place names. During their Viceregency of Ireland, 1905–15, Ishbel initiated a great revival of rural industries, especially for women. *At last we found the site for the new house at Cromar. A.[berdeen] had been looking for one for 30 years and now we discovered the perfect place ... our Highland retreat in a fashion after our own hearts, with terraces and grass walks, and an Italian garden in the midst of that wonderful panorama of hills ... There among the delectable mountains we have settled down and are writing these reminiscences.* Lady Aberdeen, 1925

The Cromar estate was bought in 1918 by Alexander MacRobert who began as a small-time clerk at Stoneywood paperworks, Aberdeen. He married an American, Rachel Workman, and made a fortune in the Indian textile industry. Sir Alexander MacRobert died in 1922, his eldest son Sir Alasdair died in a flying accident in 1933; his two younger sons, Roderic and Iain were killed in action in the RAF in 1941. Lady MacRobert gave five war planes to the government, one named *MacRobert's Reply*. She then set up the MacRobert Trust in 1943, providing money for agricultural improvement and educational benefits. She dedicated Cromar House, renamed Alastrean House after her sons and meaning *Hearth of Honour for Winged Heroes of the Stars*, as a rest home for the RAF in 1943.

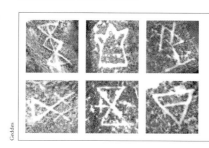

Left *Alastrean House.* Above *Whiteley Bridge, masons' marks.*

with granite margins and stringcourses. Later balustraded portico. Semicircular staircase tower similar to Drumoak, Coull and Aberdour (see *Banff & Buchan* in this series) manses. Two rear wings create a U-shaped plan.

137 **MIGVIE**
Once a separate parish. The little box **church**, *c.*1780, stands on a site of ancient significance. **Migvie Stone**, 8th century, in churchyard, an important Pictish stone, intermediate between the Class I rough boulders incised with symbols and the Class II dressed stones carved in relief with symbols and Christian motifs. This one shows a complex interlace cross, appearing to derive from textiles or metalwork, with suspension loops at the corners. Beside it are symbols: the shears, double disc and Z-rod, a horseshoe and V-rod. On both sides there is a man on horseback. Cupmarked stone next door at **The Glack** is covered with at least 40 circular indents or cupmarks, Scotland's earliest type of monumental sculpture. Opposite the church **Migvie Castle** stood with a rickle of walls until the 18th century.

Top *Corrachree*. Above *Migvie Stone*.
Right *Tillypronie*.

John Clark, as a child, was recovering from an illness at Abergeldie (next to Balmoral) when Queen Victoria was looking for a suitable Highland estate in 1847. Her doctor, Sir James Clark, recommended the climate of the upper Dee where his son was thriving, and this eventually led to the royal choice of Balmoral. Queen Victoria laid the foundation stone at Tillypronie, labouring on horseback up the long hill. She declared the house would be more appropriately named 'Kill-a-pony'! The house was designed as a modest summer lodge.

Tillypronie, 1867
Two-storey, E-plan lodge with hipped roofs over projecting bays, built for Sir John Clark, son of Queen Victoria's physician, Sir James Clark. Front hall has Jacobean style panelling and strapwork plaster ceiling. The morning, dining and drawing rooms, quite small and discrete, face the view. Long, low service wing, 1928, with a series of five gables, is in well-cut stone. An unaffected design without undue historicism, taking advantage of the outstanding view from the top of the hill.

LOGIE COLDSTONE

An ancient and secretive parish with few scattered settlements and numerous prehistoric sites skirting the east slopes of Morven. Commercial forestry and natural regeneration around Lochs Davan and Kinord clothe and conceal much of the land. Tucked behind a tight rocky cleft is the **Burn o' Vat**, nature's architecture and sculpture, a deep eroded cauldron of sheer rock, entered through a crevice and backed by an elegant cascade of water.

Deserted churchyards of the two Pictish parishes of Logie and Coldstone still survive, each with Class III stones (early Christian crosses).

Coldstone House, 1783
Two-storey-and-attic façade with canted dormers, rear section of this double-pile former manse is from the first build. Extended 1826. Attractive cast-iron balustrade on stairs.

Top *Burn o' Vat by G W Wilson.* Above *Coldstone House.* Left *Newkirk of Logie Coldstone* .

138 **Newkirk of Logie Coldstone**, from 1780
Mainly the massive rebuild of 1876 by Duguid of Ballater, the church has a substantial tower with Venetian window belvedere at the top. Converted to house, 1990s, in which the mighty bulk of the nave and offices provide space for swimming pool, upper level living room and kitchen to side. Imposing and generous.

Logie Coldstone Primary School.

Logie Coldstone Primary School, in this wooded district, has appropriately experimented with a Norwegian-style wood cabin for new classrooms, 1994.

From top *Loch Davan hut circles; Loch Kinord Pictish cross; Ferrar; Dinnet House.*

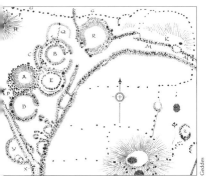

Braes of Cromar Free Church and **Manse**, 1843–4
Generous, single-storey-and-attic house, rectangular box church, with four arched windows, converted to two holiday cottages, 1990, sensitively retaining the full height of the building with bedrooms along open galleries, clad in traditional tongue-and-groove panelling.

Blelack House, from 18th century
Once owned by the Jacobite Gordons, the main block was destroyed in 1745 after Culloden. It must have been similar to Balnacraig (see p.106) with a main house and two detached single-storey wings forming a courtyard. Present three-storey-and-attic house, 1850s, unnecessarily tall, brooding and almost sinister, a gaunt and badly proportioned example of Victorian shooting-lodge structure, with mullion windows and square tower at the back. Converted into flats, 1940s.

TULLICH
The parish of Glenmuick, Tullich and Glengairn is formed by the mighty nexus of three rivers joining the Dee on the flat plain around Ballater. The three ancient and abandoned churchyards are situated roughly at the estuary of each river. Upstream from each of them, the country is wild, mountainous and sparsely inhabited. In about 1770, social and commercial focus shifted decisively to Ballater, the newly created township. The route follows the north bank of the Dee from Dinnet to upper Glengairn, via Ballater. By **Loch Davan** are the impressive hut circles, around 2000 years old, outlines of adjacent souterrains, and evidence of a ceremonial use of public space between the houses. **Loch Kinord**, 8th-century Class III Pictish stone, a dressed boulder carved in relief with complex knotted cross. Faces Castle Island, one of two crannogs in the lake.

Ferrar, 19th century
Double-pile house with possibly earlier core – house recorded here from 1298. An unusually large variation on the three-bay, two-storey farmhouse with pronounced haunched chimneys. Substantial **offices** to rear dated 1831, formerly used by the factor to Aboyne Castle.

Dinnet House, 1890, A Marshall Mackenzie
A formidable mansion for Charles Wilson MP, later Lord Nunburnholme, three storeys with massive crenellations and crowsteps above, nine-bay garden front, large gaping plate-glass sash

139

windows. Top two floors restored after 1904 fire, when square tower by front door added. Extensive west wing demolished and lofty high-pitched roof lowered, but remainder still impresses with its sheer bulk. **Lodge**, 1890s, more compact and concentrated than the big house: round tower, polygonal tower and crowstepped gable.

Dinnet Church, 1899
Quoad sacra church for Sir William Cunliffe Brooks, in the form of simple gothic box with triple lancet windows and bellcote. Boundary walls of coursed river pebbles, as at Aboyne Castle.

140 **Cambus o' May Station**, 1876
Toy Town shed, now one of the prettiest holiday cottages. Vertical wood panelling, sash windows and tile cresting on roof. The line opened in 1866 and closed in 1966; the station was mostly used to import dynamite and export quarried granite (colour p.125).

Top *Lodge, Dinnet House.* Above *WCB monogram, Dinnet Church.*

Cambus o' May Suspension Bridge, 1905, James Abernethy and Co. (colour p.124)
Suspension bridge with lattice girder pylons and parapet, one of a series of three on the upper Dee, donated by grateful local, Alexander Gordon, a brewer who settled in Kent. A graceful and elegant solution to one of the Firmounth drovers' crossings, previously negotiated by ford. Similar to **Polhollick Suspension Bridge**, Ballater, 1892.

Left *Cambus o' May Hotel.* Below *Tullich Church.*

Cambus o' May Hotel, 1874
Originally a fishing lodge, a present from William Cunliffe Brooks to his daughter Amy (see p.120). Fourteen bedrooms, coursed rusticated granite, front has triple gables, entrance through classical columns by front door.

141 **Tullich Church**, *c*.1400
Moulded north-west doorway with sculptured drip stones, rubble built rectangle, medieval and

later; abandoned 1799. Circular churchyard indicates early Christian origin, connected with the missionary work of St Nathalan. Collection of early carved stones extracted from the walls: 7th-century Class I symbol-stone with double disc, Z-rod, elephant and mirror, suggesting a pre-Christian significance for the site, and numerous other cross-marked stones, including massive boulder font.

Tullich Lodge, 1897, A Marshall Mackenzie
Boldly baronial T-plan mansion with tower in angle, coursed and squared granite with polished dressings, for William Reid, Aberdeen advocate. Stringcourses wrap around the building, tower added 1910, further additions 1923, A Vincent Harris. Good interior wood and plaster.

Above Tullich Lodge. Right Ballater Bridge.

BALLATER
Grid-plan village, begun *c.*1770 on the instigation of Francis Farquharson of Monaltrie, to provide accommodation for *strangers from a distance* who frequented Pannanich Wells (see p.131). Ballater swiftly superseded the accommodation at the old burgh of Tullich, and its foundation was consolidated by the building of the parish church in 1798, which replaced the three rural churches in glens Tullich, Muick and Gairn.

Monaltrie Hotel, Bridge Square, *c.*1860
Large Tudor building with three major stone bays and elaborate bargeboards. Opposite, leading up to the bridge, a potentially fine row of mid-19th-century houses running from the river to

Patrick Geddes, 1854–1932, the polymath and town planner, was born in Ballater. His initial studies in biology gave him a holistic view of the world, man's relationship to nature and to society. His first improvement in town planning was with the Dundee Social Union and then in the Old Town, Edinburgh. At Ramsay Garden, he set up an academics' colony, being a founder member of the Celtic Revival movement. His social planning concepts were based on an understanding of sustainable development and an awareness of society's spiritual, cultural and physical needs. He took his ideas to Cyprus, Jerusalem, Bombay, France and the United States.

Deebank Road, including the stableyard of **Cornellan Square**. Although they are the first vista of Ballater, arriving from the east, their appearance is marred by unsightly signing and street furniture. The sturdy blocks of shops along **Bridge Street** would all benefit from the 'conservation standard' of signing applied to Kincardine O'Neil (see p.107).

Ballater Bridge, 1885, Jenkins and Marr
Four segmental arches with bull-nosed cutwaters, rectangular refuges in solid parapet, pinned red ashlar. An inscription tells the story: the first bridge, providing the essential commercial link to the wells, was built 1783, destroyed 1789; the Thomas Telford bridge of 1809 was destroyed in the 'Muckle Spate' of 1829; the wooden bridge lasted from 1834 to 1885 and its foundations are still visible to the east.

142   **Riverside Cottage**, off Bridge Street, late 18th century, awaiting restoration, three swept dormers cutting the wallhead and formerly 16-pane sash windows. Joists are whole slender tree trunks, complete with bark, but in perilous condition. **9 Deebank Road**, late 19th century, has carved corbels above windows and Doric porch. **No 11**, Inchley, *c.*1830–40, hipped Scotch slate roof, coved chimneys, rustic Doric porch. The two make a handsome group facing the river.

143 **Deebank House**, Dee Street, *c.*1835
Dignified three-bay mansion of evenly coursed pink granite and shallow-pitch hipped roof with modillioned eaves. Stringcourse between floors; sandstone pilaster doorpiece.

144 **Ford House**, late 18th century
By riverbank, long and low with coved chimneys, upper windows with four panes, narrow lower windows with eight panes. One of the oldest houses in town, possibly built before the bridge.

Parish Church, Church Square, 1873–4, J Russell Mackenzie
Three-sided entrance, lower part of tower steeply battered, granite rubble. Incorporates old date stone, 1798. Very similar to Rubislaw Church in details (see *Aberdeen* in this series). The church, with its commanding steeple, presides over nearby **Victoria Road, Dee Street, Braichlie Road**, broad streets sharing a quiet uniformity of unpretentious but sturdy houses whose doors open directly onto the road, mostly after 1850, single storey with dormers.

From top Chemist, Bridge Street; *Riverside Cottage; Deebank House; Ford House; Parish Church.*

145 St Nathalan's RC Church, Golf Road, 1905, Archibald Macpherson
Snecked red granite with grey granite dressings. Three-sided apse with small windows, rather like the prow of a barge. An emphatic mass, but dark inside.

Fairways, Golf Road, 1930s
Like a migrant bird on the wrong route, this International-style echo, with whitewashed stucco walls, flat roof, angular bays and horizontal metal-frame windows, looks lost in the granite and slate of Ballater. Rare but recherché. Other semidetached 1930s' stucco cottages along this road.

146 The Barracks, Queen's Road, 1869, William Smith? Tudor holiday cottages for the royal bodyguard; symmetrical sweeping gables, yellow crested roof ridges, grey granite with pink facing, large mullion windows. An orderly arrangement of five blocks and a larger mess block, surrounded by iron railings.

Top *St Nathalan's RC Church*. Middle *Fairways*. Above *The Barracks*.

Right *Station*. Below *Albert Memorial Hall*.

147 Station Square, the scene of many royal appearances, combines Victorian civic dignity with Highland informality. **Station**, 1866, rebuilt 1886, closed 1966, happily renovated 2000, by Aberdeenshire Council as tourist office. Built of clapboard, with deep eaves forming a canopy with decorative bargeboards, also featuring on slender entrance front *porte-cochère*. Decorative leaded-glass windows. The only Royal Waiting Room in Scotland. The station was specially coloured in the Imperial livery of black and gold for the arrival of Tsar Nicholas II of Russia in 1896.

Albert Memorial Hall, 1875; **Gordon Institute** (both donated by Alexander Gordon) and **Victoria Hall**, 1895, W Duguid and Son
Unified by red granite with grey dressings, two storey with gables. Four-storey baronial tower to Albert Memorial Hall.

St Kentigern's Episcopal Church, 1907,
A Marshall Mackenzie
Snecked grey granite, north aisle of nave has
round-arched arcade on circular piers.

148 **Monaltrie House,** 1782, James Robertson
Low, two-storey, nine-bay building for Francis
Farquharson of Monaltrie. Hip roof, centre with
battlemented bow with blind side windows.
Generous tripartite windows on first floor.
Considerable offices to rear. Long elevation and
small rooms resemble the other Farquharson
inns, Pannanich Hotel and Inver Hotel (see
p.131 and p.150).

Auld Kirk Hotel, Braemar Road, early 1880s
Former Free Church, west end has gothic
entrance with two storeys of lancets below an
impressive broach steeple. Converted to hotel
by Stewart Anderson, interior divided
horizontally and an extra row of windows
added. Its re-use preserves an important
ingredient in the town's development.

Sluievannachie, Old Line Road, 1836
Single-storey-and-attic house for Peter Mitchell,
with rear wing. Moulded skewputts on gables
and pediment dormers. Attractive fanlight with
intersecting tracery. Impressive chimneystacks,
diamond coped on square base.

'Balmorality' reaches a crescendo as the **Braemar
Road** leaves town, with a series of competing
baronial mansions.

149 **Craigendarroch House,** 1869
Originally L-plan with plain gable front, by the
builder George Hall for himself, but aggrandised,
1920, by addition of square tower with balustrade
and ashlar archway in the re-entrant and finger
turret with conical roof at west end. Granite
stag's head at entrance reputedly from
Glenmuick House.

Monaltrie House.

Francis Farquharson (d.1790) was
responsible for raising troops in the Dee
valley, to support Bonnie Prince Charlie.
He fought in the front line at Culloden
and was subsequently sentenced to
death. The minister of Crathie, John
Macinnes, rode all the way to London
and successfully begged for his
reprieve. With his home at Monaltrie
(west of Balmoral) burnt, Francis began
again as an entrepreneur, developing
the wells at Pannanich, building inns
there and his new mansion in Ballater
(later known as Monaltrie House).

Below *Sluievannachie.*
Bottom *Craigendarroch House.*

St Andrew's Nursing Home
Crowstepped gables, crenellated round tower, less dressed stone than adjacent Oakhall.

150   **Oakhall**, 1890, has everything in miniature, tightly massed, crowstepped gables, round tower, square tower, pediment dormers, wandering stringcourse and even castellated 'sitooterie' on castellated terrace. **50 Braemar Road** and **Glenbardie** provide more of the same.

Darroch Learg Hotel, 1890s
Two storeys of Scottish granite, topped with very English gables covered in fish-scale tiles and overlaid with half timbering. Reminiscent of Shaw at Cragside, Northumberland.

151 **Craigendarroch Hilton**, 1891
For James M Keiller of Dundee, the marmalade manufacturer, symbolically constructed of marmalade-coloured imported sandstone, although situated next to a pink granite quarry. Surrounded by a rash of timeshare **apartments**, 1980s–90s, pink Fyfestone, black steel and glass. Stepped terraces, discretely tucked into the woods, feature a first-floor living room with extensive covered balcony, supported by either bald steel girders or a square column of Fyfestone. This site presented an exceptional opportunity to develop a new vernacular style for the woods and crags of Ballater, but the result is simply another housing estate.

Top *Oakhall*. Middle *Darroch Learg Hotel*. Above *Timeshare apartments, Craigendarroch Hilton*.

Below *Gairnshiel House*.
Bottom *Gairnshiel Bridge*.

GLENGAIRN
Abergairn Castle, 1614
Small square-plan hunting lodge, interior only 3m x 3m, with exterior stairturret in corner. Walls 1.5m thick, perhaps originally three or four storeys high. Commands a fine view at the mouth of the glen.

Gairnshiel House, late 19th century
'Shooting box', as gaunt and bleak as Corgarff Castle (see *Gordon* in this series). Double-pile core, two storey, three bay, with additional three-storey-and-dormers front wing and lower rear wing. Coursed granite and modern plate-glass windows.

152 **Gairnshiel Bridge**, 1750
Military bridge, a romantic and commanding structure, stamping order onto the wilderness with a long sweeping parapet on the south side and steep humpback. Nearby, **Kirkstyle Bridge**, 1750, small rubble segmental arch, was part of the same campaign.

153 Glenfenzie, dated 1822 on skewputt
High on the wild hills above the Gairn, this bleak
and deserted farm provides an important fixed
point for so many other similar but undateable
vernacular buildings. Long and low with massive
3m wide hearth enclosed by segmental lintel of
cut voussoirs and steeply coved chimney top
above. On opposite gable, a much smaller hearth
(*c*.1m) with a single stone lintel and a smaller
coved chimney. Machine-sawn joists and rafters
may relate to the second date carved on the front
in 1879.

154 Glengairn Parish Church, 1800
Small harled rectangle with bellcote; Georgian
Gothick windows in gable and two round-
headed windows in flank. Interior renewed.
Small and practical for a scattered settlement.

Above *Glengairn Parish Church.*
Left *Dalphuil.*

Dalphuil, 18th century
The 'Teapot House', so called because it is short
and stout, an unusually square small Georgian
former manse with hipped roofs on house, porch
and outbuilding.

155 Rineten, early 18th century
Unassuming at first glance but the details are
significant: two-storey house, harled, formerly
thatched, with irregular small windows; single-
storey wing with traditional whitewashed hearth
and swey. Its substantial steep-roofed outhouse
may have been a lordly kitchen, with majestic
hearth, massive granite jambs and lintel. Built for
the lairds, the Macdonalds of Rineten.

Rineten.

There are now no straw or heather-thatched
*roofs, but some houses still have huge
dressed-granite jambs and mantelpieces, low
fires with 'sweys' and whitewashed hearths.
Third Statistical Account,* for
Lumphanan, 1952

From top *Lochnagar Distillery; Crathie Girder Bridge; Tourist Office; Crathie Parish Church; Interior, Crathie Parish Church.*

CRATHIE AND BRAEMAR

The entire area is simply the alpine basin of the nascent Dee, cut into sections by that river's earliest affluents. The scenery of it is aggregately sublime – variously romantic, picturesque and wild (Groome, 1882). The deep valleys and waterfalls are dominated by the majestic profiles of Lochnagar, Ben Macdui, Braeriach and Cairngorm.

Lochnagar Distillery, from 1845
The seven archways for carts make an imposing entrance between two gables.
Open to the public

Crathie Suspension Bridge, 1834, J Justice Jr
Slender lattice pylons and wooden decking, partly renewed 1885, by Blaikie Bros; the original shuddering access to Balmoral. Bleats from his children led Prince Albert to commission the **Crathie Girder Bridge,** 1856–8, by Isambard Kingdom Brunel, built like a battleship to dispel all their fears.

At old **Crathie Churchyard,** little remains of the original building but the grave of John Brown (d.1883) is there, *the devoted and faithful personal attendant and beloved friend of Queen Victoria*, along with many other retainers. **Old Manse,** double-pile, rear block 1790–1; front block with pediment dormers, 1840s, possibly William Smith (see Tarland manse, p.136).

Tourist Office, Crathie, 1990s, Mike Rasmussen
Two-storey drum with conical slate roof supported on external girders. Lattice decking to balcony. Looking like a large game larder, a tactful and sensitive addition to a prominent site.

156 **Crathie Parish Church,** 1895,
A Marshall Mackenzie
Externally very simple and satisfying, interior intimate and dignified – a paradoxical compromise, where the Head of the Church of England regularly worships in a Presbyterian parish church. On site of 1805 church, square crossing tower, steep pitched gable at west end of nave, with rose window, fronted by tiled and timbered wooden porch, reminiscent of a Norwegian stave church. Rock-faced granite on the outside, interior with rustic tongue-and-groove dado panelling and wooden wagon roof. Ashlar Romanesque crossing arches. Fine wooden reredos copied loosely from the choir stall canopies, King's College Chapel (see *Aberdeen* in this series).

It was so calm and so solitary, it did one good as one gazed around; and the pure mountain air was most refreshing. All seemed to breathe freedom and peace, and to make one forget the world and its sad turmoils.
Queen Victoria, on her first visit to Balmoral, 1848

William Smith, 1817–91, son of John Smith, impressed Prince Albert with his work at Trinity Hall, Aberdeen, 1845–6, and was thereafter invited to collaborate with the prince at Balmoral (1853–5). In Aberdeen he also designed The Boys' and Girls' Hospital, the City Hospital and Rosemount Church.

Left Balmoral. Below Balmoral, before 1830s.

Balmoral, 1834–8 by James Giles.

157 Balmoral, 1853–5, William Smith and Prince Albert
The Tudor mansion by John Smith, 1834–8, for Sir Robert Gordon, had a 15th-century core. It provided the first home for Queen Victoria and her family after they leased the estate in 1848 (bought in 1852), and was demolished in 1853. The elevations of Balmoral are bold, but the detailing is bland. The most impressive view, from the west, shows the great square tower (a barrack for the menservants), 30m high, with the ballroom, west wing and extensive *porte-cochère* clustered beneath. Roofline punctured by conical corner turrets at every opportunity. The Glen Gelder stone is silver granite polished smooth (colour p.127).

The plan provides the most interesting part of the building, highlighting the Victorian fascination for hierarchy and taxonomy. Based on two linked courtyards, there are wings for royals, guests, courtiers, servants; dining rooms for three ranks of servants, rooms for coffee, lamps, silver, serving and waiting. Interiors are a bizarre mixture of medieval, Tudor and classical, originally brightened by acres of tartan (carpets, curtains, upholstery and even linoleum) and thistle wallpapers.

Prince Albert designed a model estate and the complexity of offices around the house is exceptional. **Iron ballroom**, 1851, E T Bellhouse, corrugated-iron cladding, external classical

Lady Augusta Bruce visiting Queen Victoria at Balmoral: *The carpets are Royal Stuart Tartan and Green Hunting Stuart, the curtains, the former lined with red, the same Dress Stuart and a few chintz with a thistle pattern, the chairs and sofas in the drawing room are Dress Stuart poplin. All highly characteristic and appropriate but not equally flatteux to the eye.*

Iron ballroom.

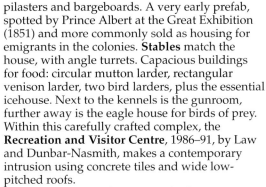

The owner-built thatched house, or 'cot stob-thackit, wi' twa timmer lums' is becoming a thing of the past. Many of the old houses, with the once familiar 'hingin lum' are also fast disappearing.
Third Statistical Account, for Logie-Coldstone, 1950

pilasters and bargeboards. A very early prefab, spotted by Prince Albert at the Great Exhibition (1851) and more commonly sold as housing for emigrants in the colonies. **Stables** match the house, with angle turrets. Capacious buildings for food: circular mutton larder, rectangular venison larder, two bird larders, plus the essential icehouse. Next to the kennels is the gunroom, further away is the eagle house for birds of prey. Within this carefully crafted complex, the **Recreation and Visitor Centre**, 1986–91, by Law and Dunbar-Nasmith, makes a contemporary intrusion using concrete tiles and wide low-pitched roofs.

Garden Cottage, from 1850s, built as a gardener's dwelling with sitting room where Queen Victoria could retreat to write her journal. Rebuilt 1890s as bland apartments, particularly for noisy grandchildren, with pine log verandas.

Dairy is an attractive octagonal with stone veranda to reduce the heat. Interior has pendant vaults, bold tile frieze and stained glass windows of simplified William Morris vegetation.

Pyramid on Creag an Lurachain, 1862 Memorial for Prince Albert, from his *broken-hearted widow*. Inscribed: *He being made perfect in a short time fulfilled a long time.*

Garbh-allt-shiel bridge, 1878, Blaikie Bros Picturesque metal-girder bridge over fine waterfall (colour p.127).

158 **Auchtavan**, *c*.18th century
Probably a lime burners' clachan, principal house has heather thatch under corrugated iron, rafters bedded half-way up the walls and timber 'hanging lum' with hearth on the floor. Smoky sleeping accommodation in loft. Two small doors and one window below, one loft window in gable. Rare survival but disintegrating fast.

Inver Hotel, from late 18th century
Coaching inn built by the Farquharsons of Invercauld; six bays, pediment dormers break wallhead. Distinctive Invercauld chimneys: polygonal, springing from canted square base. Tudor modifications from the designs of Peter Frederick Roberts, London. Chimneys later 19th century; interior refitted after 1978 fire.

159 **Old Invercauld Bridge**, 1753, Major Caulfield
Military bridge to link Blairgowrie with Corgarff and Inverness. Humpbacked, high segmented

arch with lesser arches at each side, massive V-cutwaters. Superseded in 1859 by new **Invercauld Bridge**, J F Beattie, built at the expense of Prince Albert who closed the old South Deeside commutation road between here and Balmoral in order to secure his privacy. Coursed granite with circles in spandrels.

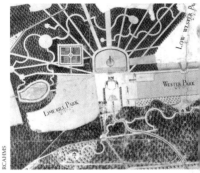

Top *Old Invercauld Bridge*. Above *Invercauld House plan, 1753*. Left *Invercauld House*.

In 1715 the Earl of Mar raised the standard of Jacobite rebellion in Braemar. The plotting for the uprising took place in the great hall of Invercauld.

Opposite from top *Stables; Garden Cottage; Dairy; hanging lum, Auchtavan*.

Below *Summerhouse, Invercauld House*. Bottom *Keiloch*.

160 **Invercauld House**, from 1750
Extended Z-plan, three-storey-and-attic wings, colossal six-storey square tower, containing around 168 rooms. Vaulted basement of tower probably 16th century. Aspect from west (as seen from the road) shows tower rising like a sheer cliff above gaunt gabled wings. Entrance front, from east, looks more like a giant Toy Town castle with separate disjointed elements stuck together: semicircular bow end with flat crenellated roof; polygonal room with pointed roof; and military entrance porch set at an angle. Additions, 1820; ogee Jacobean gables added, 1847; remodelled, 1875, by J T Wimperis, crowstepped gables added, tower raised.

In the garden, elaborate *boiserie* **summerhouse**, with (in addition to Balmoral cricket pavilion, c.1988) the only recent heather thatch to be seen in this region, 1999.

Keiloch, early 19th century
Single-storey estate cottage with hipped roof, bowed central bay; well balanced and attractive.

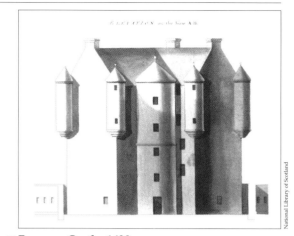

Right *Braemar Castle, 1750, from the Board of Ordnance.* Below *Braemar Castle, 2000.*

National Library of Scotland

Geddes

161 **Braemar Castle**, 1628

L-plan tower house with circular stairturret in re-entrant. Flat-topped parapets make it look oddly bald. Built for the 7th Erskine Earl of Mar as a summer residence but captured by the Farquharsons of Inverey in 1689. John Farquharson raised the standard for the 1715 revolt here. Sham Gothick crenellations and zig-zag outer wall with gunloops, 1748, as at Corgarff Castle (see *Gordon* in this series). From 1748–97 it became government barracks, interiors thus considerably stripped. *Open to the public*

BRAEMAR

Braemar provides a bizarre contrast. It combines grimly decent accommodation for Victorian tourists with a Klondike informality for the locals. The first impression is of mighty hotels and villas with overwhelming eaves and sculpted bargeboards. A closer look reveals the tiny, low and formerly thatched stone crofts scattered casually around. Canny natives added a 'wee house' usually of corrugated iron or clapboard at the bottom of the garden. This was their seasonal family retreat while they let the big house to summer visitors of a 'more select class'. The Clunie water divides two formerly separate settlements: Castleton to the east, the Farquharsons' of Invercauld Protestant village; and Auchendryne to the west, the Duke of Fife's predominantly Catholic village (colour pp.123, 124).

Fraser's Bridge, Glen Clunie, *c.*1748–50, General Blakeney

Two rubble-built segmental arches, for the Board of Ordnance, partly rebuilt 1860s. Part of the military road from Braemar to Glenshee. In its

Decent housing and agricultural improvements came slowly to Braemar. In 1790 there were no roads to the peat hags which had to be cut each summer for fuel. Tenant farmers had to use pack horses instead of carts; they had to feed more ponies than their land could bear; they had to provide the laird with a year's supply of fuel. As a result, the husbandman spent 'from seed time to harvest' shifting peat instead of spreading manure or maintaining his stone dykes. Statistical Account, 1793

splendid isolation, a poignant reminder of the suppression of the Jacobites (colour p.128).

Castleton

162 Invercauld Arms Hotel, mid-19th century
Originally a three-bay central block with projecting full-height gable porch and lower side wings. Additions have created projecting end bays and porch flanked by thimble bartizans. Timber tree-trunk columns support verandas. A good roof with oversailing eaves holds all the elements together. Extension by J T Wimperis, 1886.

163 Invercauld Church, 1832, Alexander Fraser
Dignified T-plan in yellow/brown rubble, with a serene east gable of three stepped lancets under hoodmoulds; small tower with circle of gabled lancets at base of spire; additions in stugged grey ashlar, 1878, Matthews and Mackenzie. Originally parish church, then United Free Church, then Festival Theatre, now two private apartments. The bright mural from theatre days is retained in a stairwell.

164 St Margaret's Episcopal Church, 1899–1907, Sir J Ninian Comper
Replaced a small timber church of 1880 by J B Pirie, built for the swelling numbers of English tourists, surely reminding them of home. Nave, chancel and transepts have elaborate traceried windows, constructed with a harmonious mosaic of coloured local stone. After a long bleak church-crawl through the Mearns and Dee valley, the loving detail of this interior is an inspiration, East Anglian *c.*1400, wagon roof with crenellated king-post trusses in nave; rib-vaulted crossing; carved wooden rood screen; stone wine-glass pulpit accessed by mural stair; choir stalls English perpendicular; chancel ceiling coffered with Tudor roses. Tragically weeping internally, owing to the faulty mortar mix used to repair the exterior in 1998.

Castleton Terrace, early 19th century
Attractive row of small, single-storey cottages, originally thatched, with small windows. Gives an impression of the village before it achieved royal respectability.

From top *Invercauld Arms Hotel; Invercauld Church; Interior, St Margaret's Episcopal Church; Castleton Terrace and Prince Albert's Observatory.*

Prince Albert's Observatory, 1855
Octagonal, modelled on game larder, with elaborate roof and cupola, to monitor the extremes of local climate. Braemar records the coldest temperatures of any Scottish village.

Stevenson's Cottage, mid-19th century
Incorporating gables of an earlier cottage, single
storey with dormers and Tudor-arched
doorpiece. Robert Louis Stevenson wrote
Treasure Island here in 1881.

165 **Invercauld Galleries**, Glenshee Road, 1880,
J B Pirie
Imposing two-storey former Victoria Hall with
horseshoe-arched windows below and large
pedimented windows above. Bull-faced granite
ashlar with finely tooled dressings.

Clunie Mill, 19th century
Picturesquely sited beneath the Linn, converted
to modern house.

166 **Kindrochit Castle**, foundations of tower, 1390,
later extended, ruined by 1618
On Clunie water, the castle was the bridgehead
for major routes across the Mounth and as such
has had a military significance, symbolising
royal control at the head of the Dee. The castle
is recorded here from the 11th century, and
Robert II issued charters from here 1373–82.

*Top Stevenson's Cottage and St
Margaret's Episcopal Church. Above
Invercauld Galleries.*

*From top Fife Arms Hotel; Heritage
Centre; Juniper Cottage; Wee House.*

Auchendryne
167 **Fife Arms Hotel**, *c*.1880
Large, three storey and attic, purpose built for
the 'carriage trade'. Busy gabled façade with
plenty of bay windows and castellated porch
for good measure. Grey granite with pink
dressings. Refronted and raised, 1898, A
Marshall Mackenzie; entrance porch raised and
doubled in size *c*.1905, also Mackenzie.

Heritage Centre, Fife Arms Mews,
mid-19th century
U-shaped courtyard, harled with ashlar
margins, Gothick windows on exterior. Interior
discretely modernised, 1990, John McRobert for
Grampian Regional Council, to form tourist
shops with tactfully low visual impact.

Juniper Cottage, Mar Road, mid-19th century
Important 'authentic' house, retaining original
external features including local Glen Callater
graded slate roof and outbuildings, although
reglazed and no longer harled. Gable dormers
set into wallhead, pronounced overhanging
eaves. In back yard, **Wee House**, later 19th
century, rubble stone walls, two doors, pipe flue
instead of chimney, corrugated-iron roof.

Clunie Bank, Cluniebank Road,
early 19th century
Satisfyingly elaborate T-plan, single-storey-and-attic house. Coped chimney on older wing and considerable detailing on later addition: cavetto cornice on chimneystack; Venetian window; traceried fanlights over doors; altered *c*.1840.

Left *Mill of Auchendryne, c.1900.* Below *The Granary.* Middle *Granary Cottage.* Bottom *Braemar Parish Church.*

168 **The Granary** (former Mill of Auchendryne), Cluniebank Road, 18th century
L-plan, rubble with steeply pitched slate roof, derelict mill rescued and sensitively converted to home. *It has received an extraordinary amount of attention from artists and photographers* (McConnochie).

Granary Cottage, Cluniebank Road,
late 19th century
A wee house, horizontal timber cladding, four-pane sash windows and corrugated-iron roof, sentry-box wooden porch.

Braemar Parish Church, Cluniebank Road, 1869
Early gothic former Free Church, solemnly equipped with apse, tower, spire, transepts and baptistery.

Mar Road and Auchendryne Square
169 **Auchendryne Jubilee Hall**, *c*.1897
Horizontal and diagonal red timber cladding, gay white bargeboards, drooping eaves, gable finials. Built by the Duke of Fife to rival the Invercauld Victoria Hall, symbolising the joyful relaxed aspect of this side of the village, and the competitive spirit of the Farquharson and Fife patrons (colour p.128).

St Andrew's RC Church.

170 St Andrews RC Church, 1839
Meanly narrow with four stepped buttresses at the west end and gabled bellcote. Lugubrious stained glass of Scottish saints and Bishop Chisholm, 1903. Ancient boulder stone font. Wrought-iron decorative gates at entrance, with cast-iron standards, Harper & Co. Adjacent **priest's house**, c.1870. **Humanae Vitae House**, Chapel Brae, has 1795 date stone of previous Catholic church.

Building **Braemar Catholic Church**: *It was a joyous day. They set about like men determined to do their duty. The crashing of the falling trees, the joyous shouts of the men, the bustle of the numerous horses dragging the timber, the merry pibrochs of the hardy Highlanders formed altogether as merry a scene as these hills ever witnessed… They drank the health of General Duff in a bumper of mountain dew.* John Stirtin, *Crathie and Braemar*, 1925

Hayfield, Linn of Dee Road
Low single-storey cottage with canted dormers terminates an attractive echelon of respectable Victorian villas beside Auchendryne Square: **Piedmont** and **Auchendryne Lodge**.

Beyond Braemar, the Dee forms an awesome flood plain up to the Linn of Dee (colour p.126). From here, the Mar Lodge estate extends to the Arctic tundra of the Cairngorms.

Right Mar Lodge, engraving by C Cordiner, 1780. Below Mar Lodge, before 1895 by Sir R Cotterell. Middle New Mar Lodge, before 1895 by G W Wilson. Bottom Corriemulzie game larder.

Mar Lodge, late 18th century (demolished)
Plain and sober three-storey hunting lodge for the Earl of Fife, three-windowed bow front flanked by single bay on each side. Symmetrical arrangement of single-storey plain offices to either side of the house. Damaged in 'Muckle Spate' of 1829 and eventually demolished late 19th century.

171 New Mar Lodge, or **Corriemulzie Cottage**, mid-19th century
Sensibly built higher on the valley side, out of the flood plain. Woodland style prevailed: the whole building was covered in lattice trellis, verandas and balconies with columns and balustrades made of tree trunks, bargeboards framed with antlers. Of this, the **game larder** and **keeper's cottage** survived the fire of 1895. Octagonal game larder with gothic arched door and windows and a bell-cast polygonal roof supported by rustic veranda. Harled cottage covered in a lattice screen.

Entrance to Mar Lodge over **Victoria Bridge**, 1905, lattice girder and iron horseshoe arch with inscription; handrail survives from 1848 bridge. Well-sited **gatelodge**, 19th century, is like a pug dog with an over developed and squashed nose. Stubby Ionic portico, with pink monolith columns, vastly ambitious for the tiny house.

172 **Mar Lodge**, 1895, A Marshall Mackenzie Obtuse-angled U-plan; two storey, pink rock-faced granite, mullion windows and half-timbered gables; bright orange tile roof. Its alien style is more like a German hunting lodge and it sadly misses its log column and brushwood vaulted veranda. During extensive repairs in 1991 (when all the Duke of Fife's original furniture was removed), interior of the central block was totally gutted by fire. Reception rooms are now replicas, with good wood panelling and plasterwork, rest of the house divided into holiday apartments (colour p.128).

Top Victoria Bridge and gatelodge.
Above Mar Lodge.

Below Ballroom. Bottom Inverey House.

Ballroom, 1898, retains the style of Corriemulzie, with lattice exterior and alarming quantity of deer skulls (2,500) inside, an eerie ossuary. **Stables**, a fine clean design, modestly reflecting the gables of the big house. **Episcopalian chapel**, Norman revival oblong box. *National Trust for Scotland; let to the public*

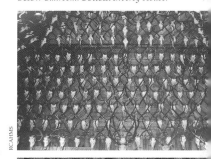

173 **Inverey House**, 1983, Oliver Humphries Deceptively authentic rooflines and proportions suggest an ancient shooting lodge but it is a modern house for Captain Ramsay of Mar. Particularly successful are the grouping of the three wings, the small size and variety of windows. Pink harling conceals modern materials underneath. Commands an outstanding

Cottages at Little Inverey by G W Wilson.

The houses *of the common people in these parts are shocking to humanity, formed of loose stones and covered with sods or with heath, broom and branches of fir; they look at a distance like so many molehills.*
Thomas Pennant, 1769

Right *Linn of Dee Bridge.* Below *Linn of Quoich.*

In the 1730s the Mar Lodge estate was purchased by William Duff (of Duff House, see *Banff & Buchan* in this series), Earl of Fife. Princess Louise, daughter of Edward VII, married Alexander Duff, 1st Duke of Fife, in 1889 and this royal connection boosted the prestige of the estate. It was sold to John and Gerald Panchaud in the 1960s as a hotel and ski centre. In 1989 it was bought by the American millionaire John Kluge. During his restorations the house was severely damaged by fire, but the main rooms are fully restored, still containing the original Fife furniture. In 1995, the house and estate were acquired by the Heritage Lottery Fund for the National Trust for Scotland for £12m in order to secure the unique and vulnerable environment of the adjacent Cairngorms which represents a greater prize for the nation than the house itself which is available for holiday lets.

view, in contrast to the adjacent **Knock Cottage**, *c.*1870, which, despite a pleasing if over-designed façade with dramatic chimneys, and dormers like the prow of an ocean liner, resolutely turns its blank back to the view.

174 **Linn of Dee Bridge**, 1857, W Reid (colour p.126) Pink granite with crenellated parapet for the Earl of Fife, leaping over the gushing torrent of the Dee where it funnels into a dramatically narrow gully.

Linn of Quoich, later 19th century
Royal picnic cottage, rustic, three timber wallhead pediments over windows and door with *boiserie* in-filling. A typical destination for royal visitors, beside a spectacular waterfall and Nature's sculpture, the Earl's Punchbowl, an odd hole in the rock (colour p.128).

Allanaquoich, *c.* 1800
Not what it seems, a lonely lopsided farm at the end of the road. It began as the seat of the Farquharsons of Allanaquoich, surrounded by a busy hamlet. Its simple exterior of asymmetrically placed windows and a lower kitchen wing belie an interior of some refinement. Doors and windows have fine architraves, a generous staircase curves around an unusually spacious hall, and principal upper room may well have been a parlour, with its lofty coved ceiling. The hidden lintel of the kitchen hearth is about 2m long.

This book has been a collaborative venture, drawing on the knowledge and enthusiasm of many friends and colleagues who deserve my grateful thanks. The text was patiently read and transformed by Charles McKean, David Walker, Norman Marr, Stuart Carrie and Ian Shepherd whose detailed local knowledge was invaluable. Ian is particularly thanked for adding a wave of euphonious adjectives as well.

Ian Begg, Alistair Urquhart, Bill Cowie, Laura Murdoch, Victoria Ball and Debbie Mays provided many essential details. The staff of Special Collections, Aberdeen University provided friendly access to the essential local library resources. Neil Gregory, Bitte Kakebeek and Sarah Blomfield helped in initial survey work. Jim Henderson generously supplied some professional photographs.

Gerda Geddes, loyal companion all the way, skilfully fielded hesitant house owners and was convinced that her aged presence at the doorstep made us look like harmless missionaries selling promises of the after life, rather than common house breakers. The book could not have been written without the interested help from so many house owners in Deeside and the Mearns who generously shared tales about their property.

Continuous moral support and practical advice came from the patient staff at the Rutland Press, Helen Leng and Susan Skinner. The flair of Adrian Hallam of The Almond Consultancy created the imaginative layout from countless boxes of messy slides.

BIBLIOGRAPHY

R Callander, **Drystane Dyking in Deeside**, 1982; Robin Callander, **History in Birse**, nos 1–4, 1985; Ronald W Clark, **Balmoral, Queen Victoria's Highland Home**, 1981; F C Diack, **A History of Glentanar**, typescript only, at Glentanar Rangers Service; Robert Dinnie, **An Account of the Parish of Birse**, (1865), 1999; W M Farquharson Lang, **The Manse and the Mansion**, 1987; A D Farr, **The Royal Deeside Line**, 1968; G M Fraser, **The Old Deeside Road**, 1921; A Gibb, **Views in Stonehaven**, 1840; F H Groome, **Ordnance Gazetteer of Scotland**, 1882; John A Henderson, **History of the Parish of Banchory-Devenick**, 1890; John A Henderson, **Annals of Lower Deeside**, 1892; J Henderson, **Scenery of the Dee** (based on the 1850s' drawings of A Gibb and J M Hay), 2000; Connie Leith, **Alexander Ellis, a fine Victorian Architect**, 1999; A I McConnochie, **Deeside**, 1900; Walter Macfarlane, **Macfarlane's Geographical Collections**, Scottish Historical Society, LI, 1906; D MacGibbon and T Ross, **The Castellated and Domestic Architecture of Scotland**, 1887–92; Delia Millar, **Queen Victoria's Life in the Scottish Highlands depicted by her water colour artists**, 1985; L Miller, **Historic Kirkyards in Kincardine and Deeside**, 1996; Thomas Pennant, **A Tour of Scotland**, 1769; Queen Victoria, **Our Life in the Highlands**, ed. A Helps, 1973; George Robertson, **A general view of the Agriculture of Kincardineshire**, (early 1800s); Sheila Sedgwick, **The Curious Years**, 1991; Sheila Sedgwick, **The Legion of the Lost**, 1999; W Douglas Simpson, **Glenbervie and its Castle**, PSAS, 105, 1972–4, 255-261; W Douglas Simpson, **The development of Dunnottar Castle**, Archaeological Journal, 1941, XCVIII, 87-98; Harry Gordon Slade, 'Arbuthnott House, Kincardineshire', PSAS, 110, 1978–80, 432-74; Robert Smith, **Valley of the Dee**, 1989; John Stirton, **Crathie and Braemar**, 1925; J Sutherland, 'The heraldic ceiling of Balbegno Castle', Aberdeen University Review, XLVI, 1975–6, 269-272; **The Statistical Account of Scotland**, XIV, 1791–9; **The New Statistical Account of Scotland**, XII, 1845; **The Third Statistical Account of Scotland**, ed. D Smith, Kincardine, 1988; ed. H Hamilton, Aberdeen, 1960; N Tranter, **The Fortified House in Scotland**, vol.4, 1986; G Walkden, **About Banchory**, 1987; B Walker, **Farm Buildings in the Grampian Region**, 1979; A Watt, **Highways and Byways around Stonehaven**, 1984; A Watt, **Highways and Byways round Kincardine**, 1985; **We Twa, Reminiscences of Lord and Lady Aberdeen**, 1925; S Wood and J Patrick, **History in the Grampian Landscape**, 1982; F Wyness, **Royal Valley, the Story of the Aberdeenshire Dee**, 1968.

For further reading on Balbridie, see Aberdeen University Review, 1982, pp.168, 238-49.

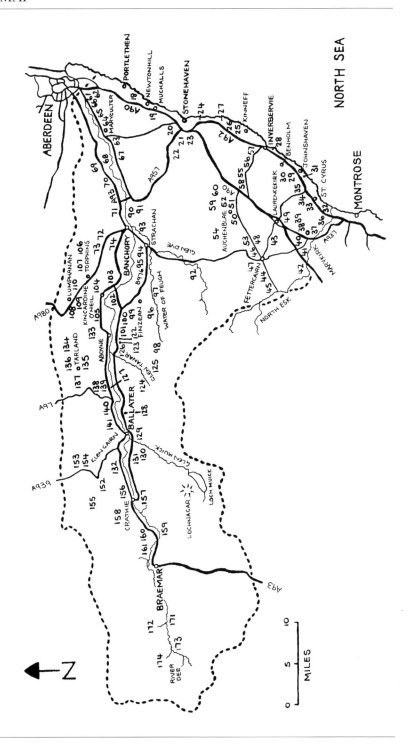

DEESIDE AND THE MEARNS

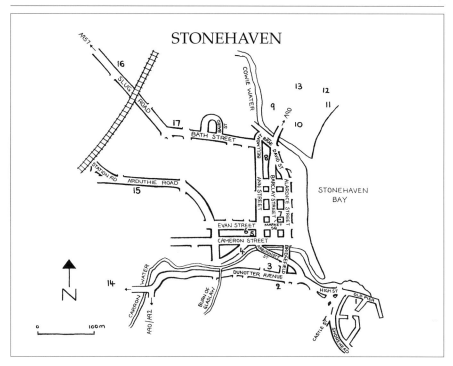

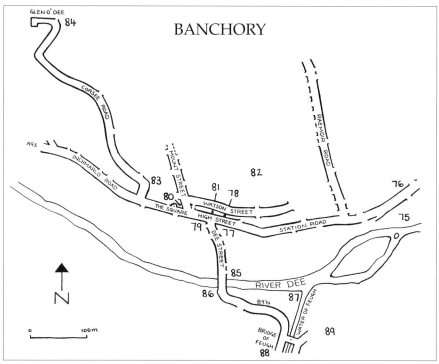

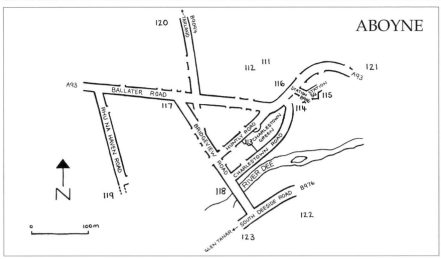

ABOYNE

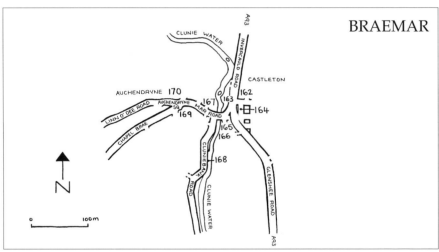

BRAEMAR

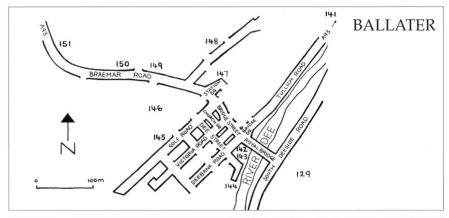

BALLATER

1. Architrave (projecting ornamental frame)
2. Astragal (glazing bar)
3. Barge (gable board)
4. Basement, raised
5. Bull's-eye, keyblocked (circular window with projecting blocks punctuating frame)
6. Buttress (supporting projection)
7. Cap-house (top chamber)
8. Cartouche (decorative tablet)
9. Cherrycocking (masonry joints filled with small stones)
10. Channelled ashlar (recessed horizontal joints in smooth masonry)
11. Chimneycope, corniced
12. Chimneycope, moulded
13. Close (alley)
14. Cobbles
15. Console (scroll bracket)
16. Corbel (projection support)
17. Crowsteps
18. Cutwater (wedge-shaped end of bridge pier)
19. Doocot, lectern
20. Dormer, canted and piended
21. Dormer, pedimented (qv) wallhead
22. Dormer, piended (see under 'roof')
23. Dormer, swept wallhead
24. Fanlight (glazed panel above door)
25. Finial (crowning ornament)
26. Fly-over stair
27. Forestair, pillared
28. Gable, wallhead
29. Gable, wallhead chimney
30. Gable, Dutch (curved)
31. Gibbs doorway (framed with projecting stonework)
32. Harling
33. Hoist, fishing net
34. Hoodmoulding (projection over opening to divert rainwater)
35. Jettied (overhanging)
36. Lucarne (small dormer on spire)
37. Margin, stone
38. Mercat Cross
39. Marriage lintel
40. Mullion (vertical division of a window)
41. Nave (main body of church)
42. Pavilion (building attached by wing to main building)
43. Pediment (triangular ornamental feature above windows etc.)
44. Portico
45. Quoins, rusticated (corner stones with recessed joints)
46. Refuge (recess in bridge parapet)
47. Ridge, crested
48. Roof, flared pyramidal
49. Roof, leanto
50. Roof, ogival (with S-curve pitch generally rising from square plan and meeting at point)
51. Roof, pantiled
52. Roof, piended (formed by intersecting roof slopes)
53. Roof, slated
54. Skew (gable coping)
55. Skewputt, moulded (lowest stone of skew, qv)
56. Skewputt, scroll
57. Stair jamb (projecting containing stairway)
58. Stringcourse (horizontal projecting wall moulding)
59. Transept (transverse wing of cruciform church)
60. Transom (horizontal division of window)
61. Voussoir (wedge-shaped stone forming archway)
62. Tympanum (area within pediment, qv)
63. Window, bay (projecting full-height from ground level)
64. Window, oriel (corbelled bay, qv)
65. Window, sash & case (sliding sashes within case)

PROMOTING ARCHITECTURE IN SCOTLAND

The Rutland Press is dedicated to producing books which stimulate awareness of Scotland's built environment in an entertaining and informative way. The publishing division of the Royal Incorporation of Architects in Scotland (RIAS), it is Scotland's leading architectural publisher with two-thirds of the series now been published in a venture unmatched elsewhere in the world.

PUBLISHED TITLES: 1. Edinburgh, 2. Dundee, 3. Stirling and The Trossachs, 4. Aberdeen, 5. The South Clyde Estuary, 6. Clackmannan & the Ochils, 7. The District of Moray, 8. Central Glasgow, 9. Banff & Buchan, 10. Shetland, 11. The Kingdom of Fife, 12. Orkney, 13. Ross & Cromarty, 14. The Monklands, 15. North Clyde Estuary, 16. Ayrshire & Arran, 17. West Lothian, 18. Borders & Berwick, 19. Gordon, 20. Sutherland, 21. Midlothian, 22. Caithness, 23. Dumfries and Galloway, 24. Perth & Kinross, 25. Deeside & The Mearns,

FORTHCOMING TITLES: 26. Falkirk and District, 27. Western Seaboard, 28. Argyll and the Islands, 29. Angus, 30. Inverness, Nairn, Badenoch & Strathspey, 31. Greater Glasgow, 32. Lanarkshire, 33. Cumbernauld, Kilsyth & the Campsies, 34. East Lothian.

THE RUTLAND PRESS

"Good armchair reading with their exotic mixture of fact and personal comment"
Colin McWilliam, *The Scotsman*

These and other RIAS books and books on world architecture are all available from RIAS Bookshops at 15 Rutland Square Edinburgh EH1 2BE Tel 0131 229 7545 Fax 0131 228 2188 email rutland@rias.org.uk website www.rias.org.uk The Rutland Press is part of RIAS Services Limited